A Friendly Guide to
The Birth of Jesus

Mary Coloe

garratt
PUBLISHING

Published in Australia by
Garratt Publishing
32 Glenvale Crescent
Mulgrave, Vic. 3170

www.garrattpublishing.com.au

Text Copyright © Mary Coloe 2017
All rights reserved. Except as provided by the Australian copyright law, no part of this book may be reproduced in any way without permission in writing from the publisher.

Design and typesetting by Lynne Muir
Images copyright © iStock

Attributions List from Creative Commons:
Page 13, Joseph the Dreamer, Battistero di San Giovanni mosaics © Marie-Lan Nguyen CC-BY 2.5
Page 10, Ruth in Boaz's field, Julius Schnorr von Carolsfeld
Page 24, Joseph and his brethren welcomed by Pharaoh, James Tissot
Page 37, The Magnificat, James Tissot
Page 48, Presentation of Jesus in the Temple, Giovanni Bellini
Page 50, Simeon's Song of Praise, Rembrandt
Page 52, Christ in the Temple, Heinrich Hofmann
Other photos by Mary Coloe

Printed and quality control in China by Tingleman

Scripture quotations are drawn from the *New Revised Standard Version of the Bible*, copyright © 1989 by the Division of Christian Education of the National Council of the Churches of Christ in the USA.

Used by permission.
All rights reserved.

Nihil Obstat: Reverend Monsignor Gerard Diamond MA (Oxon), LSS, D.Theol, Diocesan Censor
Imprimatur: Monsignor Greg Bennet, MS STL VG, Vicar General
Date: 14 July 2017
The Nihil Obstat and Imprimatur are official declarations that a book or pamphlet is free of doctrinal or moral error. No implication is contained therein that those who have granted the Nihil Obstat and Imprimatur agree with the contents, opinions or statements expressed. They do not necessarily signify that the work is approved as a basic text for catechetical instruction.

ISBN 9781925073379

Cataloguing in Publication information for this title is available from the National Library of Australia.
www.nla.gov.au

The author and publisher gratefully acknowledge the permission granted to reproduce the copyright material in this book. Every effort has been made to trace copyright holders and to obtain their permission for the use of copyright material.

The publisher apologises for any errors or omissions in the above list and would be grateful if notified of any corrections that should be incorporated in future reprints or editions of this book.

CONTENTS

INTRODUCTION 3
Ancient birth narratives 4

THE GOSPEL OF MATTHEW 9
Biblical genealogies 9
Joseph, Mary and the virgin birth 12
Fulfilling ancient prophecies 15
The history of Israel revisited 20
From Egypt to Nazareth 25

THE GOSPEL OF LUKE 27
Luke's infancy narrative 27
Canticles of Mary and Zechariah 37
The birth of Jesus 44
The circumcision and presentation in the Temple 48

CONCLUSION:
SEEKING A DEEPER MEANING 54

FURTHER READING 55

INTRODUCTION

Christmas provides us with many wonder-filled narratives. There are two in the New Testament: in the Gospels of Matthew and Luke. Apart from these, many of us carry our own Christmas narrative, with all sorts of "characters" in the Christmas story. Often when I ask adults about the Christmas narratives, I get the following mixture: Mary, Joseph, Jesus, Shepherds, Kings, an innkeeper, donkey, angels, sheep, a star, Herod, and occasionally a drummer boy! These stories, remembered from childhood, are compounded by the annual crib scene depicted in churches and sometimes even in shops, as well as various Christmas carols, songs and family traditions. I suspect that few actually read the Gospel texts to check the facts!

When I ask adults to hold a label with a character's name and to place the labels on two different sides of the room, only then do they realise that they frequently confuse the Gospels and end up with only one impossible narrative.

Luke's side would have shepherds, angels, sheep, Elizabeth, Zechariah, Mary, Joseph, Simeon, Anna and the angel Gabriel.

Matthew's side would have Joseph, Mary, some magi, King Herod, a star and an unnamed angel.

There is no innkeeper, no donkey or cows, and definitely no drummer boy.

Luke tells a joy-filled story of a birth and angels singing, "Glory to God in the highest", while Matthew tells a darker story of a man considering divorcing his spouse because she is pregnant before her marriage to him. This story then shifts to the court of King Herod, who is trying to trick some foreign visitors into revealing the birthplace of the child. This trickery is followed by a story of many young boys being murdered by Herod's soldiers.

These starkly different narratives, in their characters, symbols and writing style, have one purpose – **to introduce their readers to the adult person, Jesus of Nazareth.** If we are to read and understand these narratives, we need to have some knowledge about birth narratives in the ancient world and how different these are to the sort of birth-notice we are familiar with today.

MATTHEW 1:1–2

¹An account of the genealogy of Jesus the Messiah, the son of David, the son of Abraham. ²Abraham was the father of Isaac, and Isaac the father of Jacob, and Jacob the father of Judah and his brothers...

LUKE 1:1–3

¹Since many have undertaken to set down an orderly account of the events that have been fulfilled among us, ²just as they were handed on to us by those who from the beginning were eyewitnesses and servants of the word, ³ I too decided, ... to write an orderly account for you ...

ANCIENT BIRTH NARRATIVES

A typical birth notice today would be something like: "Tom and Nicole are delighted to announce a little sister for Owen and Josh. Lucy Patricia came a little early but weighed a healthy 3.1 kg. Nic and Lucy are doing well. Thanks to all at the Mater for your care." Such a notice appears one or two days after the birth and is a simple announcement of basic facts, not a narrative about the family, or the child, or any family difficulties.

In the ancient world, birth narratives were composed only for important people such as kings or heroes and only when they were adults, or even after they had died!

One important person who lived two thousand years ago was Caesar Augustus, who was famous as a soldier and the first Emperor of Rome. In writing his biography, a Roman historian described "omens" from the Roman gods, given before Caesar's birth and in his early years, to show that this child was destined for great things.

> When Atia [Augustus' mother] had come in the middle of the night to the solemn service of Apollo, she had her litter set down in the temple and fell asleep, while the rest of the matrons also slept. Suddenly a serpent glided up to her and shortly went away. When she awoke, she purified herself, as if after the embraces of her

Below: Augustus – signs of his greatness.

husband, and at once there appeared on her body a mark in colours like a serpent, and she could never get rid of it … In the tenth month after that Augustus was born and was therefore regarded as the son of Apollo. Atia too, before she gave him birth, dreamed that her inner vitals were borne up to the stars and spread over the whole extent of land and sea, while Octavius [Augustus father] dreamed that the sun rose from Atia's womb. (Suetonius. *The Lives of the Twelve Caesars*)

What is important to notice is that the greatness of the adult Caesar is written back into his birth and childhood. This was a standard way of beginning a biography. **Truth lies in the greatness of the *adult*** and his achievements, not in the symbols used to linked this greatness to his birth.

BIRTH NARRATIVES IN THE BIBLE

Birth stories and announcements in the Bible are similar to other ancient birth stories. Their starting point is the *adult* person, and then the adult is introduced by a birth story using symbols to show that this child is destined to have a special role in God's plan. Often the birth is presented as miraculous to emphasise that the power of God lies behind this birth. The biblical writers also have some common elements in their announcements about the future birth of a child. We never read a

DID YOU KNOW?

✦ Bedouin Arabs today look back to Ishmael as their ancestor. The Hagar episode, produced or edited hundreds of years after the events described, may be an attempt to explain the hostility between the Israelites and the Arabs trying to co-exist in the land.

Below: Bedouin preparing food on a campfire.

DID YOU KNOW?

✦ The Gospel of Mark, which was the earliest written Gospel and dates back to 70 CE, begins with the adult Jesus and adult John preparing the way for Jesus' ministry. At Jesus' baptism, the Spirit comes upon him and Jesus hears "a voice came from heaven, 'You are my Son, the Beloved'" (Mark 1:11).

✦ Ten to fifteen years later, the Gospels of Matthew and Luke push Jesus' heavenly origins back to his birth through their birth narratives.

✦ The final Gospel of John, which dates around 95 CE, pushes Jesus' divine origins back even further: "In the beginning was the Word, and the Word was with God, and the Word was God" (John 1:1).

✦ *Beer-lahai-roi* means the "Well of the Living One who sees me".

✦ The name *Ishma-el* means "God hears", and Ishmael is considered to be the ancestor of a people called Ishmaelites, who were Israel's foes.

simple statement by a woman to her husband, such as, "I am pregnant" – this is much too ordinary when a person had been an extraordinary adult.

Here is a typical announcement of the birth of a special child. The full details can be found in Genesis 16. The story begins with Abraham having no children, and so his wife, Sarah, tells Abraham to conceive a child through Hagar, Sarah's maid. But then there is trouble between the two women, and Sarah drives Hagar out into the wilderness. Then we read this announcement story.

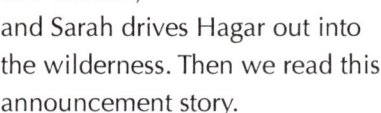

> ⁷ The angel of the LORD found her by a spring of water in the wilderness, the spring on the way to Shur. ⁸ And he said, "Hagar, slave-girl of Sarai, where have you come from and where are you going?" She said, "I am running away from my mistress Sarai." ⁹ The angel of the LORD said to her, "Return to your mistress, and submit to her." ¹⁰ The angel of the LORD also said to her, "I will so greatly multiply your offspring that they cannot be counted for multitude." ¹¹ And the angel of the LORD said to her, "Now you have conceived and shall bear a son; you shall call him Ishmael, for the LORD has heard your affliction. ¹² He shall be a wild ass of a man, with his hand against everyone, and everyone's hand against him; and he shall live at odds with all his kin." ¹³ So she named the Lord who spoke to her, "You are El-roi"; for she said, "Have I really seen God and remained alive after seeing him?" ¹⁴ Therefore the well was called Beer-lahai-roi; it lies between Kadesh and Bered. ¹⁵ Hagar bore Abram a son; and Abram named his son, whom Hagar bore, Ishmael (Genesis 16:7–15).

You might also notice the literary pattern of this announcement (although not all elements are in every announcement).

a. Appearance of an angel (or the Lord)
b. Response of fear or awe
c. Divine message –
   Person addressed by name
   Qualifying phrase describing the person
   Person urged not to fear
   Woman is to have a son
   He is to have a special name
   The meaning of his name
   His future accomplishments
   Person objects, raises a problem or expresses doubt
d. A sign of reassurance.

These elements can also be seen in the following announcement stories: the **Birth of Isaac** (Gen 17:1–21) and the **Birth of Samuel** (1Sam 1:1–28). This pattern is found in many biblical birth stories, and the Gospel writers use this pattern from the Old Testament to announce the birth of Jesus.

MARK'S GOSPEL (70 CE)

The beginning of the good news of Jesus Christ, the Son of God. ²As it is written in the prophet Isaiah, "See, I am sending my messenger ahead of you, who will prepare your way; ³the voice of one crying out in the wilderness: 'Prepare the way of the Lord, make his paths straight,'"⁴John the baptizer appeared in the wilderness, proclaiming a baptism of repentance for the forgiveness of sins (Mark 1:1–4).

DID YOU KNOW?

✦ As the New Testament developed, the story of Jesus' beginnings moved back in time from his adult life (Mark), to his birth (Luke and Matthew), to the very beginning of time with God (John).

Top: The mosaic of the Nativity, from Saint Sebastian Cathedral, Bratislava, Slovakia.

JESUS' BIRTH STORY

When we turn to Jesus and his birth story, we see something similar to the birth stories found in ancient biographies. The story of Jesus' birth was not written until well after his death. The Gospels of both Matthew and Luke are dated in the 80s CE, about fifty years after Jesus' death and around ten years after the Gospel of Mark, which was known by both evangelists and formed the "backbone" of their Gospels.

By this time, people knew a great deal about Jesus and believed that Jesus was showing the world what God was like. People were already giving him special titles, such as King, Son of God, Saviour, Emmanuel (God-with-us) and Son of David; the Jewish followers of Jesus thought he was like their great ancestor Moses. So when Matthew and Luke wrote their Gospels about the *adult* Jesus, they did not start with his adult life beginning with his baptism by John, as Mark's Gospel had. Matthew and Luke introduced Jesus by writing a birth story for him that would point to what he would be like *as an adult*.

They could simply have written the historical details, "Joseph and Mary are pleased to announce the birth of Jesus in Bethlehem."

This is the sort of birth notice we might expect today. But, considering how important Jesus was, Matthew and Luke each wanted to write a longer story about his birth that would give some clues about who this baby was going to be and what he was going to do when he grew up. As we read these stories we need to look for the clues that point ahead to the *adult* Jesus.

A GENEALOGY OF JESUS

[1] An account of the genealogy of Jesus the Messiah, the son of David, the son of Abraham.

[2] Abraham was the father of Isaac, and Isaac the father of Jacob, and Jacob the father of Judah and his brothers, [3] and Judah the father of Perez and Zerah by Tamar, and Perez the father of Hezron, and Hezron the father of Aram, [4] and Aram the father of Aminadab, and Aminadab the father of Nahshon, and Nahshon the father of Salmon, [5] and Salmon the father of Boaz by Rahab, and Boaz the father of Obed by Ruth, and Obed the father of Jesse, [6] and Jesse the father of King David.

And David was the father of Solomon by the wife of Uriah, [7] and Solomon the father of Rehoboam, and Rehoboam the father of Abijah, and Abijah the father of Asaph, [8] and Asaph the father of Jehoshaphat, and Jehoshaphat the father of Joram, and Joram the father of Uzziah,

[9] and Uzziah the father of Jotham, and Jotham the father of Ahaz, and Ahaz the father of Hezekiah, [10] and Hezekiah the father of Manasseh, and Manasseh the father of Amos, and Amos the father of Josiah, [11] and Josiah the father of Jechoniah and his brothers, at the time of the deportation to Babylon.

[12] And after the deportation to Babylon: Jechoniah was the father of Salathiel, and Salathiel the father of Zerubbabel, [13] and Zerubbabel the father of Abiud, and Abiud the father of Eliakim, and Eliakim the father of Azor, [14] and Azor the father of Zadok, and Zadok the father of Achim, and Achim the father of Eliud, [15] and Eliud the father of Eleazar, and Eleazar the father of Matthan, and Matthan the father of Jacob, [16] and Jacob the father of Joseph the husband of Mary, of whom Jesus was born, who is called the Messiah.

[17] So all the generations from Abraham to David are fourteen generations; and from David to the deportation to Babylon, fourteen generations; and from the deportation to Babylon to the Messiah, fourteen generations (Matt 1:1–17).

THE GOSPEL OF MATTHEW

Jesus and his first followers were Jews, and after Jesus' resurrection many Jews continued to be attracted to the preaching of the original disciples. Even when non-Jews (Gentiles) joined the groups of believers, it is likely that some communities were predominantly Jewish while others had more Gentile members. Scholars consider that Matthew's Gospel was particularly focused on Jewish believers, helping them to see that their past traditions, festivals and scriptures pointed the way to Jesus. Rather than abolishing the covenant and the Law (Torah) of Moses, Jesus lived as a faithful Jew, reinterpreting Jewish traditions to bring Israel's covenant to its perfection.

BIBLICAL GENEALOGIES

Matthew introduces Jesus with a very traditional literary form of a genealogy. This is a way of making links between the past and the present. In the book of Genesis, a number of genealogies establish a link from creation to Abel, then Noah, and finally Abraham. Through his genealogy, Matthew links Abraham, David and Jesus. Unlike our historical searches for ancestors through written documents, biblical genealogies were artificially created for a theological purpose. If you compare the genealogy of Jesus in Matthew and in Luke, they are not the same. Rather than be scandalised, we need to read **below the surface** and look to the intended meaning.

MATTHEW	LUKE
Jesus	Jesus
▼	▼
Joseph	Joseph
▼	▼
Jacob	Heli
▼	▼
Matthan	Matthat
▼	▼
Eleazar	Levi

CLUE 1.
MATTHEW HAS ORGANISED HIS GENEALOGY INTO GROUPS OF 14

> So all the generations from Abraham to David are fourteen generations; and from David to the deportation to Babylon, fourteen generations; and from the deportation to Babylon to the Messiah, fourteen generations (Matt 1:17).

To understand this clue to Matthew's theology it helps to know that in Hebrew, numbers are represented by letters – the first letter *aleph* stands for the number 1; the fourth letter *dalet* stands for 4; the sixth letter *vav* stands for 6. If David's name was written in Hebrew it would only have the consonants DVD – or in numbers 4–6–4, which when added together make fourteen, the name of David. So the number fourteen is a cryptic Jewish way to link Jesus to David. Joseph is called "a son of David" (1:20), and later Jesus will also be called "a son of David" (9:27; 12:23; 15:22; 20:30).

DID YOU KNOW?

✦ Even though the Bible has many references to King David, until 1993 there had been no archaeological evidence that he was a historical figure. Then, in the north of Israel at Dan, a carved stone was found with the words "House of David".

Below left: The "Star of David" is from the lintel of the Synagogue in Capernaum, possibly 3rd Century CE.

Below right: *Ruth in Boaz's Field*, by Julius Schnorr von Carolsfeld.

Opposite page: The Synagogue from Capernaum.

CLUE 2.
Look back to the genealogy and find Tamar, Rahab, Ruth, Uriah's wife (Bathsheba) and Mary

Look for a break in the pattern "X the father of Y".

If you were seeking to know your ancestors, you may not have been too pleased to find these women; all would seem to be of dubious character or involved in irregular births.

Tamar: Genesis 38

Judah had 3 sons: Er, Onan and Shelah. Tamar was the wife of Er, who died. According to Jewish Law, since Tamar had no children, her husband's brother Onan should have married Tamar so his family's seed or line could continue. He refused to give Tamar a child. Shelah was apparently too young at the time, and later Judah (Tamar's father-in-law) did not give this son to Tamar to marry. Tamar dressed like a prostitute and tricked Judah into sleeping with her and so giving her a child, Perez, of the line of Judah. While this was irregular, Judah recognised that in fact she was righteous, according to the Jewish Law.

Rahab: Joshua 2

When the Israelites escaped from Egypt, they approached Jericho and sent in spies to prepare to attack the city. The spies stayed in the house of a prostitute named Rahab, who protected them from capture. She acknowledges: "The LORD your God is indeed God in heaven above and on earth below. [12] Now then, since I have dealt kindly with you, swear to me by the LORD that you in turn will deal kindly with my family" (Josh 2:11–12). When the Israelites attacked the city, Rahab and her family were spared.

Ruth

Ruth is a Moabite, which means that she comes from a traditional enemy tribe located just across the borders of Israel. Because of a famine, a man from Bethlehem and his wife, Naomi, went to live in Moab. His sons married Moabite women, but then both sons died. Naomi returned to Bethlehem and sent her two Moabite daughters-in-law, one of whom was Ruth, back to their own people. Ruth vowed to stay with Naomi. Naomi's next of kin was a man named Boaz. Ruth tricked him into sleeping with her, and eventually Boaz married Ruth. Again this is irregular, but Boaz is next of kin to her dead husband and so Ruth acts in accord with Jewish Law. Ruth is the grandmother of Jesse the father of David.

At the end of the book of Ruth there is a short genealogy tracing the house of Judah from Perez to Boaz to Jesse to David.

Bathsheba: 2 Sam 11

Bathsheba is the wife of Uriah the Hittite. While Uriah is at battle, David sees Bathsheba bathing and sends for her, and she becomes pregnant by him. In rather comic scenes, David recalls Uriah from the battle to encourage him to sleep with Bathsheba, so it may seem that the child is his. But Uriah does not comply. Finally David sends Uriah back to the battle with a message to the General, "Set Uriah in the forefront of the hardest fighting, and then draw back from him, so that he may be struck down and die" (2 Sam 11:15). This first child dies, but then Bathsheba becomes the mother of Solomon.

These four women all have a cloud hanging over their character, yet in a mysterious way, through these four women the plan of God's promises comes about. These women are the great mothers of the line of Judah and the Royal house of David. They prepare the way for yet another woman who is found to be pregnant in an irregular way, another woman through whom the house of David will be fulfilled:

> and Jacob the father of Joseph the husband of **Mary**, of whom Jesus was born, who is called the Messiah (Matt 1:16).

These verses of the genealogy, which possibly seem boring to modern readers, would bring delight to Matthew's community. They establish Jesus' credentials as a son of Abraham, as one of the children of Israel through Judah, and belonging to the house of David. They also point to the many times in Israel's history when women have played such a significant part, even if at times they became pregnant in an irregular or scandalous manner – and yet through them and the child they bore, God's plan unfolded.

ANNUNCIATION TO JOSEPH

[18] Now the birth of Jesus the Messiah took place in this way. When his mother Mary had been engaged to Joseph, but before they lived together, she was found to be with child from the Holy Spirit. [19] Her husband Joseph, being a righteous man and unwilling to expose her to public disgrace, planned to dismiss her quietly. [20] But just when he had resolved to do this, an angel of the Lord appeared to him in a dream and said, "Joseph, son of David, do not be afraid to take Mary as your wife, for the child conceived in her is from the Holy Spirit. [21] She will bear a son, and you are to name him Jesus, for he will save his people from their sins."

[see vv 22–23 at right]
[24] When Joseph awoke from sleep, he did as the angel of the Lord commanded him; he took her as his wife, [25] but had no marital relations with her until she had borne a son; and he named him Jesus (Matt 1:18–21; 24–25).

JOSEPH, MARY AND THE VIRGIN BIRTH

Jesus' birth narrative begins with a problem – while not yet married to Joseph, Mary is "found to be with child from the Holy Spirit" (Matt 1:18). While the readers have this information about the Holy Spirit, Joseph doesn't. In Jewish marriage customs there would be a delay of twelve months after the initial betrothal, which would ensure the virginity of the bride. If Mary is pregnant, Joseph would naturally presume adultery, and he would have every right to bring a fatal punishment to her; instead he plans a quiet divorce, as he is described as "righteous".

JOSEPH—THE DREAMER

At this point, Joseph's dilemma is solved when he has a dream in which he is informed by an angel, who follows the script of an announcement story.

> Joseph, son of David, do not be afraid to take Mary as your wife, for the child conceived in her is from the Holy Spirit. She will bear a

FIRST SCRIPTURE CITATION

MATTHEW 1:22–23	ISAIAH 7:14
All this took place to fulfil what had been spoken by the Lord through the prophet:	
"Look, the virgin (*parthenos*) shall conceive and bear a son, and they shall name him Emmanuel", which means, "God is with us."	Look, the *young woman* (ălmā) is with child and shall bear a son, and shall name him Immanuel.

TIMELINE

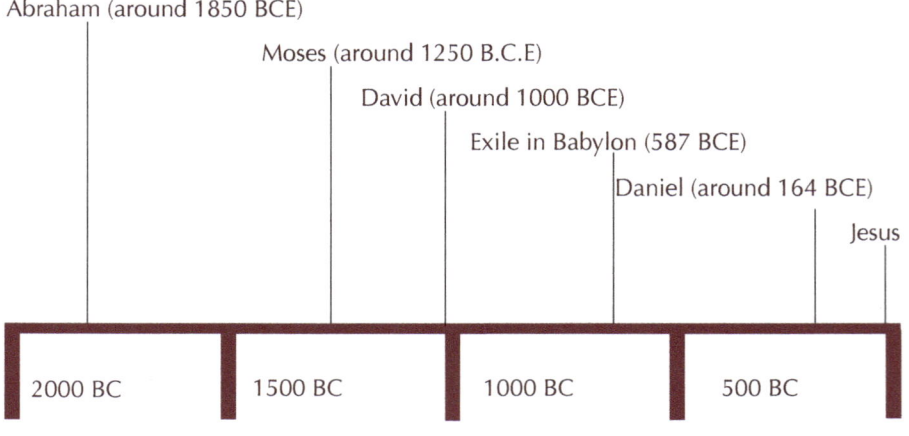

Opposite page: Joseph the dreamer, mosaic from Battistero di San Giovanni.

son, and you are to name him Jesus, for he will save his people from their sins (Matt 1:20–21).

The name "Jesus" or "Jeshuah" means "God saves", so this is what this child's mission will be: to bring God's salvation. This announcement is then supported by a quotation from Israel's scriptures.

In fact, Matthew emphasises the virginity of Mary to assure the reader that this birth is through the power of God. The original quotation from Isaiah in Hebrew refers to a *young woman* (ặlmā), and there is no claim that this young woman is a virgin, simply that she is young and of marriageable age. A change occured when the Hebrew text was translated into Greek and the "young woman" became "a virgin" (*parthenos*). So Matthew follows the Greek Old Testament (called the Septuagint) in his quotation. If you look back at some of the Old Testament announcement stories, it is often the case that the woman is old or barren. These descriptions testify to the miraculous power of God in these births.

THE VIRGIN BIRTH

Joseph responds in obedience; "he took her as his wife, *but* had no marital relations with her *until* she had borne a son; and *he named him* Jesus" (Matt 1:24–25).

There are two important things to notice in Joseph's response. The fact that he named Jesus means he accepted him as his son; we would consider this the moment of "adoption". If Joseph had refused to name him, it would indicate his rejection of this child.

The other point is the preposition "until" (*heōs*). This could be read in an absolute or general sense. In Greek and Semitic languages, when used with a negative (no ... until), the preposition "until" can have the absolute sense to mean that Joseph had no sexual relations

DID YOU KNOW?

✢ Herod, known as the Great, was appointed by Caesar Augustus to be the vassal King of the Jews in 37 BCE. He was renowned for his extensive program of building cities in a Greco-Roman style, and in order to gain favour with the Jews he rebuilt the Jerusalem Temple, doubling its size and giving employment to many over decades.

✢ Jesus was born during the rule of Herod the Great. Herod died in 4 BCE and left his kingdom to three of his sons: Archelaus, Philip and Antipas (see p14).

DID YOU KNOW?

✦ Archelaus, born around 27 BCE, ruled the largest area of Judea, Samaria and Idumea until 6 BCE, when he has dismissed and this territory became a Roman province.

✦ Philip, born around 26 BCE, ruled over the mainly Gentile territory East of the Jordan River.

✦ Herod Antipas was born around 25 BCE and ruled the territory of Galilee and Perea. Jesus' adult ministry began during his rule.

with Mary *until and beyond* the birth of Jesus. This gives rise to the title, "Mary, ever-virgin", which is a long-standing tradition, documented in an early non-canonical Gospel the *Protoevangelium of James* (about 130 CE). In this text, Joseph was a widower who already had children, and these were known as the "brothers and sisters" of Jesus. Later, the great biblical scholar and translator Jerome (born about 347 CE) wondered if the term "brethren" referred to the "cousins" of Jesus, since this is allowed in the Jewish idiom. In the ancient tribal world, the "father's household" was far broader than the modern nuclear family.

At the time of the Protestant Reformation, the early Reformers accepted this view of Mary's perpetual virginity. Later reformers moved away from this belief to understand the term "brothers" as direct blood brothers of Jesus, assuming Mary and Joseph resumed normal marital relations following the birth of Jesus. The Greek preposition "until" (*heōs*) can be interpreted in this general sense. Today, the Catholic teaching, also accepted by some Protestant Churches, is that Jesus is the only child of Mary, justifying her title of "Mary, ever-virgin".

Matthew's concern is to emphasise the power of God at work and the fulfilment of an ancient prophecy; questions about Mary's perpetual virginity belong to a later era.

This first chapter has established Jesus' Jewish lineage. He is one of the children of Abraham; he belongs to the tribe of Judah and is born into the royal House of David. In the next chapter, through its symbols, he will live out the pattern of Moses: Israel's great teacher, lawgiver and covenant maker.

Below: Mary and Jesus from the Church of the Nativity, Bethlehem.

FULFILLING ANCIENT PROPHECIES

MAGI AND STARS

Chapter two begins in the royal court of Herod the Great, recognised by Rome as the King of the Jews. Unbeknown to Herod, a child, belonging to the royal House of David, has been born in Bethlehem, where David had his origins.

¹ The LORD said to Samuel, "How long will you grieve over Saul, seeing I have rejected him from being king over Israel? Fill your horn with oil, and go; I will send you to Jesse of Bethlehem, for I have provided for myself a king among his sons." … ⁴ Samuel did what the LORD commanded, and came to Bethlehem. …⁵And he sanctified Jesse and his sons and invited them to the sacrifice. … ¹⁰ Jesse made seven of his sons pass before Samuel, and Samuel said to Jesse, "The LORD has not chosen any of these." ¹¹ Samuel said to Jesse, "Are all your sons here?" And he said, "There remains yet the youngest, but he is keeping the sheep." And Samuel said to Jesse, "Send and bring him; for we will not sit down until he comes here."¹² He sent and brought him in. Now he was ruddy, and had beautiful eyes, and was handsome. The Lord said, "Rise and anoint him; for this is the one." ¹³ Then Samuel took the horn of oil, and anointed him in the presence of his brothers; and the spirit of the Lord came mightily upon David from that day forward (1 Sam 16:1, 4, 5, 10–13).

THE MAGI MEET HEROD

In the time of King Herod, after Jesus was born in Bethlehem of Judea, wise men *(magi)* from the East came to Jerusalem, ² asking, "Where is the child who has been born king of the Jews? For we observed his star at its rising, (or in the East) and have come to pay him homage." ³ When King Herod heard this, he was frightened, and all Jerusalem with him; ⁴ and calling together all the chief priests and scribes of the people, he inquired of them where the Messiah was to be born. ⁵ They told him, "In Bethlehem of Judea; for so it has been written by the prophet: ⁶ "And you, Bethlehem, in the land of Judah, are by no means least among the rulers of Judah; for from you shall come a ruler who is to shepherd my people Israel'" (Matt 2:1–6).

THE MAGI GREET JESUS

⁷ Then Herod secretly called for the wise men and learned from them the exact time when the star had appeared. ⁸ Then he sent them to Bethlehem, saying, "Go and search diligently for the child; and when you have found him, bring me word so that I may also go and pay him homage." ⁹ When they had heard the king, they set out; and there, ahead of them, went the star that they had seen in the East, until it stopped over the place where the child was. ¹⁰ When they saw that the star had stopped, they were overwhelmed with joy. ¹¹ On entering the house, they saw the child with Mary his mother; and they knelt down and paid him homage. Then, opening their treasure chests, they offered him gifts of gold, frankincense, and myrrh. ¹² And having been warned in a dream not to return to Herod, they left for their own country by another road (Matt 2:7–12).

Opposite page: Magi from Sant Appollinare, Ravenna. Over centuries the symbolism of the magi and star from the book of Numbers was lost when non-Jews read these narratives without knowing the Old Testament. Matthew's original Jewish audience would appreciate the symbolic references to Moses and David. Later, people imagined the magi as three astrologers from Persia and even gave them names! The legend of "the Three Kings" was popular in Medieval art; however, it is not part of Matthew's text.

Herod learns of this royal birth from foreigners called "magi", or wise ones who practised the art of astrology. The magi are presented as foreigners (gentiles), who bring to fulfilment the promise to Abraham that all nations, both Jews and non-Jews, will be blessed through him.

> Now the LORD said to Abram, "Go from your country and your kindred and your father's house to the land that I will show you. ² I will make of you a great nation, and I will bless you, and make your name great, so that you will be a blessing. ³ I will bless those who bless you, and the one who curses you I will curse; and in you all the families of the earth shall be blessed" (Gen 12:1–3).

MIDRASH

At this point you need to know what type of literature you are reading. In Chapter one, the evangelist used the form of a genealogy to connect Jesus to the great leaders of Israel. In this chapter, a new form of Jewish biblical writing is introduced, called "midrash". This is a way of connecting the present to the past as a means of understanding what God is doing *now*. Previous scriptures are reread and reinterpreted to show a deeper meaning that had been obscured in the past. Look at, for example, Matthew's writings of magi and a star. If we do not understand this way of Jewish writing, we might think he is writing about a real star and look back in ancient texts for a comet or supernova. This is a mistake. If we want to understand about the magi and the star, we don't look up to the night sky but back into the scriptures of Israel.

The episode that lies behind this scene is taken from the time of Moses, when he is leading the Israelites from slavery in Egypt into the land of their ancestors. This long journey takes him over to the East to the countries of Edom and Moab.

When Moses tries to bring the people through the land of Moab, Balak, the King of Moab, objects to this invasion of refugees and calls on Balaam, his court magician – in Greek called a "*magus*". This magus is told to curse Moses and his followers:

> Thus says Balak son of Zippor: … come, curse this people for me (Numbers 22:6–7).

But instead of cursing the Israelites, Balaam speaks oracles of blessing. His final oracle states:

THE ORACLE OF BALAAM (NUMBERS 24:15–19)

> The oracle of Balaam son of Beor,
> the oracle of the man whose eye is clear,
> ¹⁶the oracle of one who hears the words of God,
> and knows the knowledge of the Most High,
> ¹⁷I see him, but not now;
> I behold him, but not near—
> a star shall come out of Jacob,
> and a sceptre shall rise out of Israel;
> it shall crush the borderlands of Moab,
> and the territory of all the Shethites.
> ¹⁸Edom will become a possession,
> Seir a possession of its enemies,
> while Israel does valiantly."

The star and sceptre are symbols of kingship; the lands mentioned in Balaam's oracle were conquered by the armies of David. These words in the book of Numbers were written much later to show that David was acting with the blessing of God – we might call it good propaganda. The oracle, supposedly from the time of Moses but pointing ahead to the victories of David, is now reinterpreted by Matthew to point to Jesus. Since most Christians are unaware of midrash and how it works, and are also unfamiliar with Israel's scriptures, we do not readily see the hidden depths in the Gospel writing. But Matthew's original audience, being Jewish, would have appreciated and grasped this symbolic reference to "magi" and "star". They would perceive in this a reference to the claims about the adult Jesus as "king" and also his links to Moses and David.

When Herod consults the priests and scribes in Jerusalem to find out where the Messiah is to be born, they name Bethlehem, the city of David.

SECOND SCRIPTURE CITATION

MATTHEW 2:5–6	MICAH 5:2
"In Bethlehem of Judea; for so it has been written by the prophet: 'And you, Bethlehem, in the land of Judah, are by no means least among the rulers of Judah;	But you, O Bethlehem of Ephrathah, who are one of the little clans of Judah,
for from you shall come a ruler who is to shepherd my people Israel.'"	from you shall come forth for me one who is to rule in Israel… "…For some time, while Saul was king over us, it was you [David] who led out Israel and brought it in. The LORD said to you: It is you who shall be shepherd of my people Israel, you who shall be ruler over Israel" (2 Sam 5:2).

DID YOU KNOW?

✦ Myrrh was used as medicine and perfume, both for sacred anointing and anointing dead bodies. It was a very precious resin from trees found in Yemen, Somalia, Arabia and India. Myrrh was mixed with spices to make a sacred anointing oil to anoint the Tent where Moses and God met and the Ark of the Covenant.

✦ Frankincense was a prized incense prepared from the gum of several shrubs native to the Arabian Peninsula. In Exodus there is a recipe using frankincense with other spices to make an incense to "be regarded by you as holy to the Lord" (Exod 30:37).

✦ Along with the gold, these gifts point ahead to the royal holiness of the adult Jesus.

Here Matthew combines the prophets Micah and Samuel to provide a citation to show that Jesus' birth in Bethlehem is the fulfilment of ancient prophecies. To shepherd is a synonym for Israel's kingship. Not only was David remembered as the young shepherd of Bethlehem, but Moses also likened his leadership to the role of a shepherd. As his time was nearing an end he asked: ^{16} "Let the Lord, the God of the spirits of all flesh, appoint someone over the congregation^{17} who shall go out before them and come in before them, who shall lead them out and bring them in, so that the congregation of the Lord may not be like sheep without a shepherd" (Num 27:16–17).

Matthew will apply this same image to Jesus when he has compassion on the crowds:

When he saw the crowds, he had compassion for them, because they were harassed and helpless, like sheep without a shepherd Matt (9:36).

GIFTS OF GOLD, FRANKINCENSE, AND MYRRH

The foreign magi from the East with their gifts recall the prophetic words of Isaiah and the Psalms, which spoke of the coming of the Gentiles to worship with the Jewish people in Jerusalem.

Nations shall come to your light,
and kings to the brightness of your dawn.

Top: Myrrh and frankincense.

Bottom: A frankincense tree.

⁴Lift up your eyes and look around;
they all gather together, they come to you; …
⁵Then you shall see and be radiant;
your heart shall thrill and rejoice,
because the abundance of the sea shall be brought to you,
the wealth of the nations shall come to you.
⁶A multitude of camels shall cover you,
the young camels of Midian and Ephah; all those from Sheba shall come.
They shall bring gold and frankincense,
and shall proclaim the praise of the Lord (Isaiah 60: 3–6).

May the kings of Sheba and Seba bring gifts.
¹¹May all kings fall down before him, all nations give him service
(Psalm 72:10–11).

Within the story of Jesus' birth, the sign is there that the Gospel is for all nations. The final command Jesus gives his disciples is, "Go therefore and make disciples of all nations" (Matt 28:19).

Much later, Christian tradition will develop Matthew's midrash and make the magi into kings, and from the number of gifts will presume there were three and further develop the legends. We need to appreciate the rich symbolism of these birth narratives if we are to read them as adults.

In the Gospel, this symbolic story has the theological importance of presenting Jesus against the background of Moses and David and also revealing that Jesus' mission is for all people. The midrash form used by Matthew interprets Jesus' adult life and then projects these insights back into his infancy – as was the custom both in Jewish and Greco-Roman biographies. This would have been grasped by Matthew's original Jewish audience, familiar with this type of interpretation of their scriptures. Unfortunately, later Christian traditions lost sight of this Jewish background and read these images in a literal sense, making up legends and carols about "the three (?) kings" travelling over "fields and mountains" to follow the star.

Below: A shepherd leading his flock as a king is meant to "lead" his people.

JOSEPH WARNED

¹³ Now after they had left, an angel of the Lord appeared to Joseph in a dream and said, "Get up, take the child and his mother, and flee to Egypt, and remain there until I tell you; for Herod is about to search for the child, to destroy him." ¹⁴ Then Joseph got up, took the child and his mother by night, and went to Egypt, ¹⁵ and remained there until the death of Herod. This was to fulfil what had been spoken by the Lord through the prophet, "Out of Egypt I have called my son" (Matt 2:13–15).

THE HISTORY OF ISRAEL REVISITED

JOSEPH—DREAMER AND SAVIOUR

When the magi depart, a much darker narrative unfolds with the threat of Herod. Once again, Joseph is presented as a man of dreams and also as the saviour of his family by taking them to Egypt.

In the background is the narrative of Joseph, the son of Jacob/Israel who was favoured by his father and given a long-sleeved robe. This led to the jealousy of his brothers. Joseph had a number of strange dreams about his superiority, which further irked his brothers, who planned his death but then sold him as a slave. He ended up in Egypt, where his dreams saved the people of Egypt from a long famine and he won great rewards from the Pharaoh. As his family also experienced famine, the brothers came to Egypt seeking grain and did not recognise Joseph. Eventually Joseph revealed himself, and all his family, including his father, came down to Egypt. For many years these children of Israel prospered. (Read this long saga about Joseph in Genesis 37–50.)

HEROD'S REACTION

Caution is needed in reading the next passage, often called "The Massacre of the Innocents". This is not a historical event but once again Matthew's midrashic reinterpretation of Israel's story, specifically the infancy of Moses, in the light of Jesus.

Moses was remembered as the great teacher and saviour of Israel. Yet his birth story, also more legend than fact, tells of a wicked king, the Pharaoh of Egypt, ordering the death of all newborn baby boys (Exod 1). This is a new Pharaoh "who did not know Joseph" (Exod 1:8) and did not favour the growth of the Israelites within his nation. The shrewdness of the midwives and Moses' mother and sister protected him, attesting to the power of God at work in the birth of Moses.

THIRD SCRIPTURE CITATION

Once again Matthew is retelling Israel's ancient story in the light of Jesus. As the children of Israel had their founding story in the great Exodus when they left Israel, now, in Jesus' birth narrative, he and his family retrace the path of his ancestors and thus fulfil the words of the prophet cited by Matthew:

MATTHEW 2:15	HOSEA 11:1
"Out of Egypt I have called my son."	When Israel was a child I loved him, and out of Egypt I called my son.

Opposite page: On the coast of the Mediterranean, Herod built a magnificent Greco-Roman city named Caesarea Maritime. It had a theatre, a hippodrome for chariot racing, a private pool and an extensive harbour reaching out in the waters.

ORDER TO KILL THE CHILDREN

[16] When Herod saw that he had been tricked by the wise men, he was infuriated, and he sent and killed all the children in and around Bethlehem who were two years old or under, according to the time that he had learned from the magi. [17] Then was fulfilled what had been spoken through the prophet Jeremiah: [18] "A voice was heard in Ramah,
wailing and loud lamentation,
Rachel weeping for her children;
she refused to be consoled,
because they are no more"
(Matt 2:16–18).

According to the legend, Pharoah's daughter found the child and so Moses grew up as an Egyptian in Pharoah's palace. Remember that birth narratives were developed in the light of the adult. Perhaps this legend was needed to expain how the greatest leader of Israel had an Egyptian name, similar to a number of Pharoahs: Thutmose, Ahmose. The birth narrative in Exodus explains the mystery about the origins of Moses.

A first century Jewish historian, Josephus, describes the cruelty and ruthlessness of Herod (74 BCE–4 CE), who had his wife and a number of his children murdered lest they compete with him for power. Josephus even describes that Herod had ordered many of the leading men of Judea to be slaughtered when he died, so that there would be weeping at his death. And yet, Josephus has no mention of Herod ordering the massacre of children, which, had it occurred, would add to his portrayal of a savage King.

Through the citation from Jeremiah, Matthew recalls another significant aspect of Israel's history: the Exile in Babylon.

Rachel was the chosen wife of Jacob/Israel whose first son was Joseph and second son was Benjamin. In giving birth to Benjamin, Rachel died, "and she was buried on the way to Ephrath, that is, Bethlehem" (Gen 35:19). Jacob marked her death with a pillar that was later associated with the village of Ramah on the main road just north of Jerusalem. At the time when Jerusalem fell to the armies of Babylon (586 BCE), Ramah was the point where the caravans of Exiles and troops gathered before setting off for Babylon (Jer 40:1). Jeremiah imagines Rachel, weeping for the children of Israel as they pass her

tomb heading into Exile.

Through these scripture citations, Matthew has retold the history of Israel – the Exodus under the leadership of Moses, the Kingdom of David, and the Exile in Babylon.

In this way, he presents Jesus as the summation of God's saving power at work in Israel and now at work in Jesus. What we need to recognise in this birth narrative is a rich theology about the adult Jesus.

FOURTH SCRIPTURE CITATION

Within Matthew's narrative of Jesus' birth, he has traced aspects of Israel's history, Bethlehem the city of David (Matt 2:6), Egypt (Matt 2:15) with its allusions to the Exodus, and the slaughter of the children in Bethlehem, reminiscent of Moses' infancy. Following the narrative of Herod's slaughter of the children in Bethlehem, a citation is added from the prophet Jeremiah.

MATTHEW 2:18	JEREMIAH 31:15
"A voice was heard in Ramah, wailing and loud lamentation,	Thus says the LORD: A voice is heard in Ramah, lamentation and bitter weeping. Rachel is weeping for her children;
Rachel weeping for her children; she refused to be consoled, because they are no more."	she refuses to be comforted for her children, because they are no more.

HEROD'S DEATH

He [Herod] commanded that all the principal men of the entire Jewish nation ... should be called to him. ... He ordered them all to be shut up in the hippodrome, and sent for his sister Salome, and her husband Alexas, and spoke thus to them: "I shall die in a little time, ... but what principally troubles me is this, that I shall die without being lamented, and without such mourning as men usually expect at a king's death." ... He desired therefore, that as soon as they see he hath given up the ghost, they shall place soldiers round the hippodrome, ... they shall give orders to have those that are in custody shot with their darts; and that this slaughter of them all will cause the honour of a memorable mourning at his funeral. (Josephus: *Jewish Antiquities* 17.174–78).

Above: Rachel's tomb as it is today.

Opposite page: Moses found in the Nile by Pharoah's daughter, from the Cathedral of Brussels.

JOSEPH TAKES FAMILY TO NAZARETH

[19] When Herod died, an angel of the Lord suddenly appeared in a dream to Joseph in Egypt and said, [20] "Get up, take the child and his mother, and go to the land of Israel, for those who were seeking the child's life are dead." [21] Then Joseph got up, took the child and his mother, and went to the land of Israel. [22] But when he heard that Archelaus was ruling over Judea in place of his father Herod, he was afraid to go there. And after being warned in a dream, he went away to the district of Galilee. [23] There he made his home in a town called Nazareth, so that what had been spoken through the prophets might be fulfilled, "He will be called a Nazorean" (Matt 2:19–23).

DID YOU KNOW?

✦ A Nazirite was a person consecrated or set apart for God. This could be a temporary vow or a life-long status. Their long hair was an outward sign of their consecration to God.

Top: *Joseph and his brethren welcomed by Pharoah*, by James (Jacques) Tissot.

FIFTH SCRIPTURE CITATION

MATTHEW 2:23

There he made his home in a town called Nazareth, so that what had been spoken through the prophets might be fulfilled, "He will be called a Nazorean."

POSSIBLE LINKS

To Samson:
Judges 13:5
"…for the boy shall be a nazirite to God from birth. It is he who shall begin to deliver Israel from the hand of the Philistines."

Judges 16:17
"I have been a nazirite to God from my mother's womb."

To someone consecrated:
Isaiah 4:2–3
On that day the branch of the LORD shall be beautiful and glorious. Whoever is left in Zion … will be called holy.

FROM EGYPT TO NAZARETH

The final episode in Matthew's infancy narrative is a description of Joseph, learning again through a dream that Herod is dead and so it is safe to leave Egypt and return home. This episode also provides the reason why he left Judea, where so far all the action has taken place, to live in Galilee and establish his household in Nazareth. In the Gospel narrative, the adult Jesus was known as "Jesus of Nazareth" (Matt 4:13; 21:11; 26:71). With Jesus settled in Nazareth, the adult life of Jesus can now begin.

This move to Nazareth is also interpreted as the fulfilment of Scripture.

This fifth citation to fulfil the prophets is unclear. There is no place in the Old Testatment that exactly matches the words, "He shall be called a Nazorean". It may be a reference to the Messiah with the symbolic name "Branch", which in Hebrew can be written with the three consonants *nzr* (originally Hebrew did not write the vowel sounds). Alternatively, it may refer to one like Samson, who is consecrated/ holy from his birth. Even before his birth, Samson is named as the one to deliver Israel from its enemies.

> "Out of Egypt I have called my son."
>
> Matthew 2:15

THE NUMBER FIVE

The fact that there are five Scripture citations may have been a deliberate allusion to Moses, whose authority lies behind the first five books of the Old Testament, known as the Torah or Pentateuch (five teachings).

In the Gospel narrative, Jesus will deliver *five* great sermons or instructions, as noted at the end of his teachings (5:1–7:29; 10:1–42; 13:1–52; 18:1–35; and 24:1–25:46); there are also references to *five* mountains (4:8; 5:1; 8:1; 14:23; 15:29).

WHAT DO WE NOW KNOW ABOUT THE ADULT JESUS?

Using the literary style of a genealogy, we can expect that the adult Jesus will in some way live out belonging to the House of David. He will speak of a Kingdom. But this will bring him into conflict with the power of Rome, for Tiberius Caesar is considered King in Israel, and for the Jewish people even Herod is allowed by Caesar to have the nominal title, "King of the Jews".

Using the literary style of a midrash, we can expect that the adult Jesus will be like Moses: that he will be a teacher and also teach new commandments; that he will inaugurate a "new Covenant".

On the "outside", the rich symbolic story of Jesus' birth contains the truth on the "inside" as long as we can read it correctly and recognise the symbols, episodes and patterns from the Old Testament.

Below: Mt Tabor. Some consider this to be the Mount of the Transfiguration.

THE GOSPEL OF LUKE

LUKE'S INFANCY NARRATIVE

Luke tells a very different birth story to Matthew. Of course, the historical details are the same: Mary, Joseph, Bethlehem, King Herod and Nazareth. But where Matthew told the story of Jesus' birth to present him as a person like Moses who was born into the royal House of David, Luke uses other Old Testament stories to show that Jesus has come to bring good news to those who are poor or outsiders – the "little people" – rather than the great important people. Remember, writers have their readers in mind. Matthew's readers were probably Jews who had come to believe in Jesus. Luke's readers were probably non-Jews (Gentiles). Writing for different readers, these evangelists needed to emphasise different aspects of Jesus' life and ministry and use different symbols that their readers would understand. Matthew uses the scriptures of Israel very obviously with the five fulfilment citations. Luke also makes use of the Old Testament but with greater subtlety.

The author of this Gospel makes it clear that he had not known Jesus but is relying on the testimony of eyewitnesses. He proposes to present an orderly account and, as a good historian should, he claims to have investigated everything carefully. This is the style of an ancient historiography, well suited to the Greco-Roman world. Scholars consider that Luke was probably a Gentile familiar with the Old Testament, perhaps one of the Gentiles attracted to Judaism and considering conversion.

THE WORLD OF LUKE'S COMMUNITY – AROUND 80–85 CE

It can help us read ancient literature if we have a sense of the world at that time and enter imaginatively into that world of the first audience.

Historically, the author is writing for a community who are third and fourth generation Christians and who only know about Jesus through

> ### LUKE'S INTRODUCTION
> Since many have undertaken to set down an orderly account of the events that have been fulfilled among us, [2] just as they were handed on to us by those who from the beginning were eyewitnesses and servants of the word, [3] I too decided, after investigating everything carefully from the very first, to write an orderly account for you, most excellent Theophilus, [4] so that you may know the truth concerning the things about which you have been instructed (Luke 1:1–4).

DID YOU KNOW?

✦ Many of Luke's non-Jewish listeners would have been very familiar with the Old Testament stories.

✦ We know that many in the Greco-Roman world were attracted to Judaism, even if they did not undergo full conversion. These Gentiles went regularly to the Synagogue, probably followed Jewish dietary laws and celebrated Jewish festivals.

✦ When Paul preaches in the Synagogues, it is some of these non-Jews who are particularly attracted to his teaching.

✦ In the Acts of the Apostles, these non-Jews are called "God-fearers" (Acts 10:2,11; 13:43; 16:4). Acts 13:42–52 shows these "God-fearers" welcoming Pauls' words.

Right: A large Torah scroll being carried.

Opposite page: The menorah used in the Festival of Hanukkah superimposed against the Western Wall of the Temple Mount in Jerusalem.

earlier eye-witnesses and through the first Gospel of Mark, written around 70 CE, and possibly the Gospel of Matthew, around 80 CE. By this time, Jerusalem has been destroyed. There is no longer a temple, no longer a system of sacrifice within Judaism, no longer a priesthood. Gathered now under the Rabbis, Judaism is in a process of self-definition. In this context, there is conflict with those who present a different form of Judaism, one proclaiming that the promises have been fulfilled in Jesus of Nazareth. The horrific destruction of Jerusalem also raises questions of, "Why?" Why was Jerusalem, the centre of so many of God's promises to Israel, destroyed? Has God been faithful to Israel?

Socially, Christians are living within the complex world of a Greco-Roman society. As Judaism and Christianity begin the slow process of clearer self-definition leading to eventual separation, Christians no longer find themselves under the protective umbrella of Judaism, with its status as a legitimate religion. Rome may be asking, "Who are these Christians? Are they a valid religious group or a set of rebels proclaiming a king to rival Caesar?"

In the light of these concerns, the purpose of the Gospel can be expressed as follows.

1. THEODICY
The Gospel was written to show that God is faithful and has kept faith with the promises made to the people of Israel. This is why there is such an emphasis on the fulfilment of prophecy.

2. PASTORAL RESPONSE TO THE DELAY OF THE PAROUSIA
The Gospel was written to deal with issues concerning how Christians are to live within their social context while waiting for the final return and triumph of Jesus Christ. This is why the Gospel exhorts the community to pray; this is why it emphasises issues of justice, inclusivity, hospitality and treatment of the poor.

3. CHRISTOLOGY
What was the mission of Jesus and why was he rejected by so many within Judaism? Given Christian faith that Jesus of Nazareth was God's Messiah, why was it that so many within Israel did not recognise him? What divine purpose lies behind his rejection by Israel and acceptance by the Gentiles?

While these themes are evident in Luke's two volumes, the Gospel and Acts of the Apostles, they are also present in the manner of Luke's infancy narrative to set the scene for the adult Jesus. By the time the reader meets the adult Jesus, they should be prepared to know how his Gospel will unfold, through reading the infancy narratives.

THE STRUCTURE OF LUKE'S INFANCY NARRATIVE

Chapters one and two show a highly crafted theological introduction to the identity and mission of Jesus. There are many characters: Zechariah, Elizabeth, Mary, Joseph, shepherds, angels, Simeon and Anna. But all these characters, so typical of Israel's traditions, are cast against a background of world powers – Caesar Augustus, Quirinius and Herod. This birth is no myth. It is grounded in history and prepared for within the long history of Israel.

LUKE:

1:5–25 Annunciation of John   26–38 Annunciation of Jesus

39–56 Meeting of the two mothers

OLD TESTAMENT RECOGNISES THE NEW

57–80 Birth and circumcision of John the Baptist   2:1–21 Birth and circumcision of Jesus

22–40 Presentation in the temple

OLD TESTAMENT RECOGNISES THE NEW

2:41–52 Bridge to public ministry
Jesus imbibing and being nurtured by the wisdom of Israel

This annunciation is typical of the pattern found in the Old Testament for the birth of a special child.

Can you identify these elements?
a. Appearance of an angel (or the Lord)
b. Response of fear or awe
c. Divine message –
   Person addressed by name
   Qualifying phrase describing the person
   Person urged not to fear
   Woman is to have a son
   He is to have a special name
   The meaning of his name
   His future accomplishments
   Person objects, raises a problem or expresses doubt
   A sign of reassurance.

Who is the prophet named?
Who is the angel named?

Below: A carved image of the seven-branched candlestick, the menorah, and other important instruments for the temple sacrifices. On the left is a small shovel used to collect incense and place it on the incense altar within the Holy Place; on the right is the shofar, which is a ram's horn that is blown like a trumpet blast. It was Zechariah's turn to offer the incense. This is from the lintel of the Synagogue of Capernaum.

THE ANNUNCIATION TO ZECHARIAH

[5] In the days of King Herod of Judea, there was a priest named Zechariah, who belonged to the priestly order of Abijah. His wife was a descendant of Aaron, and her name was Elizabeth. [6] Both of them were righteous before God, living blamelessly according to all the commandments and regulations of the Lord. [7] But they had no children, because Elizabeth was barren, and both were getting on in years.

[8] Once when he was serving as priest before God and his section was on duty, [9] he was chosen by lot, according to the custom of the priesthood, to enter the sanctuary of the Lord and offer incense. [10] Now at the time of the incense offering, the whole assembly of the people was praying outside. [11] Then there appeared to him an angel of the Lord, standing at the right side of the altar of incense. [12] When Zechariah saw him, he was terrified; and fear overwhelmed him. [13] But the angel said to him, "Do not be afraid, Zechariah, for your prayer has been heard. Your wife Elizabeth will bear you a son, and you will name him John. [14] You will have joy and gladness, and many will rejoice at his birth, [15] for he will be great in the sight of the Lord. He must never drink wine or strong drink; even before his birth he will be filled with the Holy Spirit. [16] He will turn many of the people of Israel to the Lord their God. [17] With the spirit and power of Elijah he will go before him, to turn the hearts of parents to their children, and the disobedient to the wisdom of the righteous, to make ready a people prepared for the Lord." [18] Zechariah said to the angel, "How will I know that this is so? For I am an old man, and my wife is getting on in years." [19] The angel replied, "I am Gabriel. I stand in the presence of God, and I have been sent to speak to you and to bring you this good news. [20] But now, because you did not believe my words, which will be fulfilled in their time, you will become mute, unable to speak, until the day these things occur" (Luke 1:5–20).

THE ANNUNCIATION TO ZECHARIAH

Luke's infancy of Jesus begins by introducing John the Baptist, and this establishes a pattern: John, then Jesus. In the Old Testament we see this pattern in Moses, who is followed by Joshua (in Greek this is similar to the name *Jesus*), who led the Israelites into the Promised Land, and also the prophet Elijah followed by Elisha, who was given a twofold portion of the Spirit given to Elijah.

What appears to be a very simple announcement story to Zechariah in fact reveals Luke's interest in history, particularly the Jewish idea that when things get very bad, God will bring this world's history to an end in order to destroy evil and establish a new reign of God. This rather strange worldview is called "apocalyptic", and it is found in the Book of Daniel and the Book of Revelation. Luke has used many phrases from the book of Daniel, and of particular interest is his introduction of Gabriel – who is only found in the book of Daniel.

THE BOOK OF DANIEL	LUKE'S GOSPEL
9:21 ...while I was speaking in prayer, the man Gabriel, whom I had seen before in a vision, came to me in swift flight at the time of the evening sacrifice.	1:10–11 Now at the time of the incense offering... there appeared to him (Zechariah) an angel of the Lord, standing at the right side of the altar of incense.
10:12 "...your words have been heard..."	1:13 "... your prayer has been heard."
8:16; 9:21 Gabriel 7:16 I approached one who stood in the presence of God.	1:19 The angel replied, "I am Gabriel. I stand in the presence of God,
10:11 ...I have been sent to you.	and I have been sent to speak to you and to bring you this good news."
8:17 ... when he came, I became frightened... 10:12 He said to me, "Fear not Daniel..."	1:12–13 When Zechariah saw him, he was terrified; and fear overwhelmed him. 13 But the angel said to him, "Do not be afraid, Zechariah..."
10:15 I turned my face toward the ground and was speechless.	1:20 "... you will become mute, unable to speak, until the day these things occur."
9:23 "...you are greatly beloved." 10:11 "Daniel, greatly beloved, ..."	1:28 (To Mary) "Greetings, favored one!"
10:16 ... and I opened my mouth to speak...	1:64 Immediately his mouth was opened and his tongue freed, and he began to speak, praising God.
7:28 ...but I kept the matter in my mind. (literally in my heart – *en kardia*)	2:19 But Mary treasured all these words and pondered them in her heart.

Daniel was written at a time when the Jewish people were being greatly oppressed by their Greek rulers, about 170 BCE. During this time of oppression, the hope developed that surely God would act and destroy evil and then recreate a new world order in which God's desires would be effective.

> ²⁴ Seventy weeks are decreed for your people and your holy city: to finish the transgression, to put an end to sin, and to atone for iniquity, to bring in everlasting righteousness, to seal both vision and prophet, and to anoint a most holy place. ²⁵ Know therefore and understand: from the time that the word went out to restore and rebuild Jerusalem until the time of an anointed prince [in Greek a *Christos*], there shall be seven weeks; and for sixty-two weeks it shall be built again with streets and moat, but in a troubled time. ²⁶ After the sixty-two weeks, an anointed one [*christos*] shall be cut off and shall have nothing, and the troops of the prince who is to come shall destroy the city and the sanctuary. Its end shall come with a flood, and to the end there shall be war. Desolations are decreed. ²⁷ He shall make a strong covenant with many for one week, and for half of the week he shall make sacrifice and offering cease; and in their place shall be an abomination that desolates, until the decreed end is poured out upon the desolator (Daniel 9:24–27).

Look at the significant time indicators in this passage:

> A total of 70 weeks of years
> = 70 x 7
> = 490 years
> before the end-time.

This involves 7 weeks of building, then 62 weeks of trouble, then in the 70th week the *christos* will come.

In the Old Testament, seven represents completeness or fulfilment since that is all the time it took God to create the world (Genesis 1:1–2:4). If seven is significant, then 70 times 7 symbolises utter perfection and completion. The Book of Daniel, written around 170 BCE, looks back to the time when the Temple was rebuilt after the Exile and then to the many years of struggle under foreign powers. Daniel offers hope to the people experiencing oppression by the Greek rulers that soon God's anointed one, the *Messiah* or *Christos*, will come. Luke finds in this book symbols and images that he can use to interpret what has happened in his own lifetime, first through the coming of Jesus, called "the *christos*" by believers, then with the destruction of Jerusalem and its Temple by the Romans.

The book of Daniel provides Luke with a way of interpreting Jesus' death and the destruction of Jerusalem. The believers, especially the Jewish believers, should not be surprised by these events; they were spoken of in the Old Testament. The scriptures of Israel had said that the anointed one would be "cut off" and then Jerusalem would be destroyed.

By introducing an angel named Gabriel and announcing the birth of John in a pattern similar to the Book of Daniel, Luke crafts his infancy narrative to show the deeper meaning of Jesus' death, and also the destruction of Jerusalem, as a sign that the prophecies are being fulfilled and God's reign is beginning. God is faithful!

DANIEL	PARALLELS IN THE 1ˢᵀ CENTURY
The restoring and building of Jerusalem	Herod's building program restoring the Temple
The coming of the anointed one	Jesus called the anointed one (*Christos*)
The city and its sanctuary will be destroyed	Destruction of Jerusalem by Rome (70 CE)

DID YOU KNOW?

✦ The word *"angelos"* is the Greek word for a messenger.

✦ In the Old Testament we find the names of three angels – look up Daniel 8:16; 10:18–21; Tobit 5:4

✦ Gabri–el means in Hebrew "the mighty one of God" (El means God).

✦ Micha–el means in Hebrew "who is like God".

✦ Rapha–el means in Hebrew "the healing power of God".

Below: A model of the temple rebuilt by Herod.

THE ANNUNCIATION TO MARY

26 In the sixth month the angel Gabriel was sent by God to a town in Galilee called Nazareth, 27 to a virgin engaged to a man whose name was Joseph, of the house of David. The virgin's name was Mary. 28 And he came to her and said, "Greetings, favored one! The Lord is with you." 29 But she was much perplexed by his words and pondered what sort of greeting this might be. 30 The angel said to her, "Do not be afraid, Mary, for you have found favor with God. 31 And now, you will conceive in your womb and bear a son, and you will name him Jesus. 32 He will be great, and will be called the Son of the Most High, and the Lord God will give to him the throne of his ancestor David. 33 He will reign over the house of Jacob forever, and of his kingdom there will be no end." 34 Mary said to the angel, "How can this be, since I am a virgin?" 35 The angel said to her, "The Holy Spirit will come upon you, and the power of the Most High will overshadow you; therefore the child to be born will be holy; he will be called Son of God. 36 And now, your relative Elizabeth in her old age has also conceived a son; and this is the sixth month for her who was said to be barren. 37 For nothing will be impossible with God." 38 Then Mary said, "Here am I, the servant of the Lord; let it be with me according to your word." Then the angel departed from her (Luke 1:26–38).

THE ANNUNCIATION TO MARY

Once again, to show that Jesus is no ordinary person, a messenger from God comes to announce his birth. Where Matthew focused on Joseph, Luke gives more importance to Mary, who is the first of the "little ones" to hear this good news from God. Luke emphasises that God is beginning a new creative action in continuity with God's action from the beginning of time. As the Spirit of God hovered over the water at creation, now this child will be conceived through the overshadowing of the Spirit, and later the same Spirit of God will hover over the disciples at the beginning of the Church at Pentecost (Acts 2:1-4).

The virginal conception of Jesus is similar, though not identical, to God's action in Israel where a number of women thought to be unable to bear a child (e.g. Sarah, Rachel, Hannah) become pregnant and give birth to a son who furthers Israel's salvation (Isaac, Joseph, Samuel). The purpose in the overshadowing Spirit and the virginal conception is to introduce the greatness of Jesus, called Son of the Most High, Son of David, ruler of the House of Jacob. These lofty titles are in keeping with first century Jewish expectations of a Davidic Messiah to fulfil God's promises to Israel (2 Sam 7:11–14). Mary is then given a sign verifying Gabriel's announcement in that her cousin Elizabeth is now six months pregnant, in her old age, adding the words, "Nothing is impossible with God." Mary responds in complete faith and obedience, speaking of herself as God's handmaid or servant.

> ### MEETING OF ELIZABETH AND MARY
>
> ^{39} In those days Mary set out and went with haste to a Judean town in the hill country, ^{40} where she entered the house of Zechariah and greeted Elizabeth. ^{41} When Elizabeth heard Mary's greeting, the child leaped in her womb. And Elizabeth was filled with the Holy Spirit ^{42} and exclaimed with a loud cry, "Blessed are you among women, and blessed is the fruit of your womb. ^{43} And why has this happened to me, that the mother of my Lord comes to me? ^{44} For as soon as I heard the sound of your greeting, the child in my womb leaped for joy. ^{45} And blessed is she who believed that there would be a fulfilment of what was spoken to her by the Lord."
> ^{56} And Mary remained with her about three months and then returned to her home (Luke 1:39–45; 56).

Opposite page: *The Annunciation* is by Afro-American artist Henry Ossawa Tanner (1859–1937) and is held in the Philadelphia Museum. He captured something of the fragility and wonder of a young girl just coming into puberty and the mystery Luke records.

Left: Sculpture of Elizabeth and Mary in the village of Ein Kerem, just outside Jerusalem.

DID YOU KNOW?

✦ The language of the Holy Spirit "overshadowing" Mary, and the mention that Mary stayed for three months with Elizabeth, suggests that Luke has in mind the imagery of the Ark of the Covenant. In the Old Testament, the cloud of God's Glory "overshadowed" the Tabernacle in the Wilderness, which housed the Ark (Exod 40:35). The wings of the cherubim overshadowed the Ark itself (Exod 25:20).

✦ Before David brought the Ark into Jerusalem, it remained for three months in the hills of Judea, just as Mary spent three months in the Judean hill country (2 Sam 6:6–11).

Having written about the annunciation of John the Baptist's birth and the Annunciation of Jesus' birth, now Luke brings both mothers together. Through this meeting, in the words of Elizabeth, Luke establishes that Jesus is greater than John is, and Mary is considered more blessed than Elizabeth is. According to Luke's time schema, John is the last of the prophets of Israel and he gives way to the time of Jesus.

> The law and the prophets were in effect until John came; since then the good news of the kingdom of God is proclaimed…(Luke 16:16).

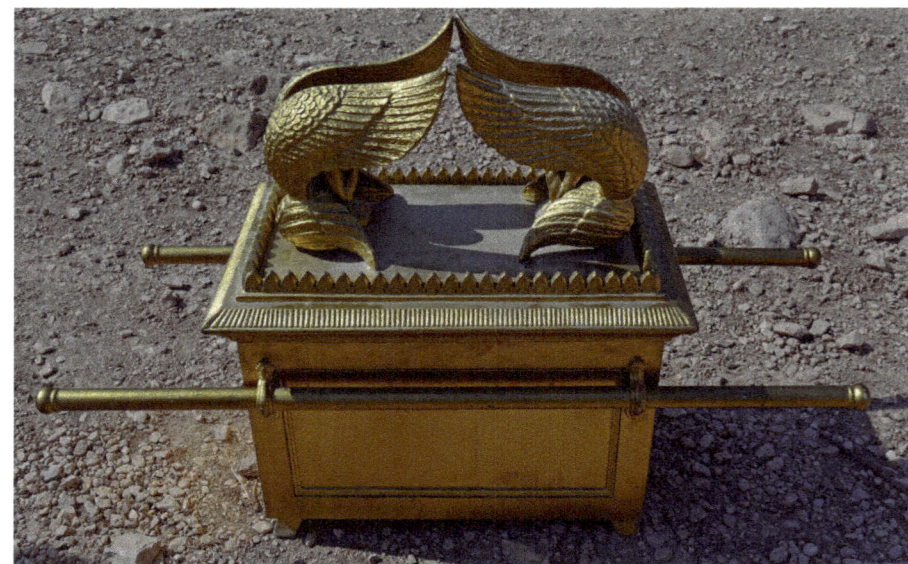

Top: Recreation of the winged Ark of the Covenant.

Middle: Ceremony of the holy ark in Ethiopia.

Bottom: This carving of the Ark of the Covenant was once part of a frieze along a lintel in the Synagogue of Capernaum, a much more important village than Nazareth. Capernaum sat on a crossroad beside Lake Galilee.

CANTICLES OF MARY AND ZECHARIAH

MARY'S SONG OF PRAISE

In response to Elizabeth, Mary sings out, "My soul magnifies the Lord, and my spirit rejoices in God my Savior…" (Luke 1:46–47).

This is the first of three great Canticles in the Lukan infancy narrative. Its theme is the marvels God has done for Mary. This Canticle, also know as the Magnificat, is very similar to the song of Hannah following the birth of her son, Samuel.

Many scholars consider that Mary's Canticle originated among the Jewish disciples of Jesus, long before the writing of Luke's Gospel. The Canticles are songs of faith in God and praise for all God does, particularly for the "little ones" or "the poor ones" (in Hebrew the *anawim*). The sentiments expressed in the Canticles can be found in many of the trusting Psalms of Israel – "O Lord, my heart is not proud, nor haughty my eyes" (Ps 131:1). This piety is placed on the lips of Mary, a young girl from a small village in Galilee.

HOPE AND PROTEST

Mary's song speaks of both spiritual and real hunger. It is the song in which the proud and mighty are toppled and the "poor ones", the oppressed, are raised. Considering that Luke's Gospel was written when Roman armies had only recently destroyed Jerusalem (70 CE), slaughtered thousands and dragged off many into captivity, this is a powerful song of hope and protest. In spite of everything, God will prevail.

Beneath the piety of the *anawim* lies quite a dangerous "subversive" song of protest.

The British-backed East Indian Company banned the Magnificat in 1805, lest it threaten their power and profits in India.

In Argentina, the Mothers of the Disappeared (*Mothers of the Plaza de Mayo*) would

> ## MARY'S CANTICLE OF PRAISE – THE MAGNIFICAT
> ### (LUKE 1:46–55)
>
> 46 And Mary said,
> "My soul magnifies the Lord,
> 47 and my spirit rejoices in God my Saviour,
> 48 for he has looked with favour on the lowliness of his servant. Surely, from now on all generations will call me blessed;
> 49 for the Mighty One has done great things for me,
> and holy is his name.
> 50 His mercy is for those who fear him
> from generation to generation.
> 51 He has shown strength with his arm;
> he has scattered the proud in the thoughts of their hearts.
> 52 He has brought down the powerful from their thrones, and lifted up the lowly;
> 53 he has filled the hungry with good things,
> and sent the rich away empty.
> 54 He has helped his servant Israel,
> in remembrance of his mercy,
> 55 according to the promise he made to our ancestors,
> to Abraham and to his descendants forever."

Left: *The Magnificat*, by James Tissot.

gather to protest against the military junta who had imprisoned their children without trial from the late 1970s. The women were banned from praying the Magnificat in these gatherings. Some of these mothers also "disappeared".

In Guatemala, the Magnificat was banned as a public or group prayer in the 1980s.

Mary's Canticle brings the first section of Luke's infancy narrative to a close. The next section tells the story of the births, first of John the Baptist and then of Jesus. Further canticles are sung, and more surprises are in store.

Right: The Mothers of the Plaza have gathered for 40 years in protest against the government.

HANNAH'S SONG (1 SAM 2:1–10)	MARY'S SONG (LUKE 1:46–55)
"My heart exults in the Lord; my strength is exalted in my God…	"My soul magnifies the Lord,
Talk no more so very proudly, let no arrogance come from your mouth;…	and my spirit rejoices in God my Savior, for he has looked with favor on the lowliness of his servant.
The bows of the mighty are broken, but the feeble gird on strength.	He has shown strength with his arm; he has scattered the proud in the thoughts of their hearts.
Those who were full have hired themselves out for bread, but those who were hungry are fat with spoil.	…he has filled the hungry with good things, and sent the rich away empty.
He raises up the poor from the dust; he lifts the needy from the ash heap,…"	He has helped his servant Israel, in remembrance of his mercy, according to the promise he made to our ancestors, to Abraham and to his descendants forever."

THE BIRTH AND CIRCUMCISION OF JOHN THE BAPTIST

The actual birth of Elizabeth's child is told very simply; the only unresolved issue is what name he will be given. Zechariah had been told to name him "John" (1:13). As a firstborn son it would be more usual to name him Zechariah, but Elizabeth says, "He is to be called John" (1:60). In disbelief of her words, the neighbours turn to Zechariah. Will he break with his family tradition, as his friends say to Elizabeth, "None of your relatives has this name." Zechariah, still mute, writes on a slate, "His name is John", and this act of submission to the words of Gabriel frees his tongue.

The rite of circumcision on the 8th day is attributed to Abraham as a sign of the covenant he made with God. Through this rite, a Jewish male is brought into the life of Judaism. By naming the child, Zechariah affirms him as his own. While the ritual is needed to affirm the father-son relationship and thus make the child one of the children of Abraham, the natural process of birth affirms the child's mother, and Judaism is passed on through the Jewish mother, who is considered "naturally circumcised" and in no need of a rite.

DID YOU KNOW?

✦ In modern times, some Jewish communities have a covenant ceremony for girls in a foot-washing ritual, recalling Abraham washing the foot of his guests who came to announce the birth of Isaac (Gen 18:4).

✦ Circumcision was common among other surrounding groups such as in Edom, Moab and Ammon.

✦ The number eight took on the symbolism of a "new creation". God took seven days for the original creation, and the eighth day is the first day of a new creation. We find this symbolism in Christian writings in the Resurrection account of John's Gospel and also in the epistle of Barnabas (Ca. 95–135).

Above: *The Circumcision in the Temple,* by Riofrio, Avila, Spain.

Right: Eight-sided baptism font in Bethlehem.
"Not the Sabbaths of the present era are acceptable to me, but that which I have appointed to make the end of the world and to usher in the eighth day, that is, the dawn of another world. This, by the way, is the reason why we joyfully celebrate the eighth day – the same day on which Jesus rose from the dead." (Ep. Barn 15.8–9)
This symbolic rebirth on the eighth day is visually expressed in many baptism fonts, which have eight sides.

THE BIRTH AND CIRCUMCISION OF JOHN THE BAPTIST

⁵⁷ Now the time came for Elizabeth to give birth, and she bore a son. ⁵⁸ Her neighbours and relatives heard that the Lord had shown his great mercy to her, and they rejoiced with her.

⁵⁹ On the eighth day they came to circumcise the child, and they were going to name him Zechariah after his father. ⁶⁰ But his mother said, "No; he is to be called John." ⁶¹ They said to her, "None of your relatives has this name." ⁶² Then they began motioning to his father to find out what name he wanted to give him. ⁶³ He asked for a writing tablet and wrote, "His name is John." And all of them were amazed. ⁶⁴ Immediately his mouth was opened and his tongue freed, and he began to speak, praising God. ⁶⁵ Fear came over all their neighbours, and all these things were talked about throughout the entire hill country of Judea. ⁶⁶ All who heard them pondered them and said, "What then will this child become?" For, indeed, the hand of the Lord was with him (Luke 1:57–66).

"What then will this child become?"

The question asked by the neighbours is a reminder to modern readers that the focus of an infancy narrative is the adult. These narratives are not historical descriptions of "what happened" but need to be read as theological introductions to the Gospel of the adult Jesus and the adult John.

All Gospels present John as one preaching the imminent arrival of the reign of God and using water immersion as a ritual seeking a return to the covenant and forgiveness. Such a ritual bathing was not uncommon within Judaism, but when linked to John's preaching along the Jordan, it attracted followers.

Since at this time some within Judaism were expecting the Messiah, they may have thought that John was this end-time Messiah figure. John was eventually killed by Herod, but his followers continued, and it seems that the early Jesus believers needed to clarify John's role.

The Gospels quite clearly emphasise that John was not the Messiah, but his role was like that of Elijah: to prepare the way. "Lo, I will send you the prophet Elijah before the great and terrible day of the LORD comes" (Mal 4:6).

This establishes the Gospel pattern of first John, then Jesus.

Paul meets followers of John the Baptist

> Paul passed through the interior regions and came to Ephesus, where he found some disciples. ² He said to them, "Did you receive the Holy Spirit when you became believers?" They replied, "No, we have not even heard that there is a Holy Spirit." ³ Then he said, "Into what then were you baptized?" They answered, "Into John's baptism." ⁴ Paul said, "John baptized with the baptism of repentance, telling the people to believe in the one who was to come after him, that is, in Jesus." ⁵ On hearing this, they were baptized in the name of the Lord Jesus (Acts 19:1–5).

DID YOU KNOW?

✦ Paul met followers of John the Baptist in Ephesus on one of his missionary journeys.

✦ Today the followers of John are known as Mandaeans, and some have settled in Australia.

Opposite page: Baptism of Jesus in the Jordan river, Ravenna.

Below: Jordan river (left); an Icon of John the Baptist.

THE CANTICLE OF ZECHARIAH

Zechariah's great song of praise, like the Magnificat, is not considered to be original to Luke but was most likely a Jewish-Christian hymn within the early community of believers. Nothing in the Canticle speaks directly about John's future ministry. There is no mention of his ministry of immersion, nor was John considered to be in the line of David since his father, Zechariah, was a priest belonging to the tribe of Levi. It was most likely composed within Jewish Christian circles pointing to Jesus as the one who fulfils the prophecies and longings of Israel. As in the Magnificat, there is strong sense of trust in God, reflecting the piety of the *anawim*, the "little ones" who have no power to save themselves "from our enemies, and the hand of all who hate us" (Luke 1:71).

The hymn has the following structure:

Below: Today there is a church on Mt Olives called Dominus Flevit – the Lord Weeps.

Opposite page: Masada's fortress, Judean wilderness.

INTRODUCTION
Blessed be the Lord God of Israel.

Verse 1: 68–71
God has *visited* God's people to raise up a Davidic saviour as promised. The term "visited" in the Greek world has the sense of an overseer (*episkopos*) or ruler who comes to inspect the city or nation. This inspection can lead to gracious action and kindness, or it could lead to displeasure and punishment. In Jesus, God has come to Israel. In the life of the adult Jesus, this is made clear in 7:16 when the crowd "glorified" God in response to a healing miracle, saying, "A great prophet has risen among us!" and "God has visited the people!" Then when Jesus approaches Jerusalem to look down upon from Mt Olives, he weeps over it. Luke knows of the destruction of Jerusalem in 70 CE and so presents Jesus lamenting this event and, in Luke's theology, interpreting this destruction as punishment on Jerusalem for not recognising God's visitation and rejecting Jesus.

> [41] As he came near and saw the city, he wept over it, [42] saying, "If you, even you, had only recognized on this day the things that make for peace! But now they are hidden from your eyes. [43] Indeed, the days will come upon you, when your enemies will set up ramparts around you and surround you, and hem you in on every side. [44] They will crush you to the ground, you and your children within you, and they will not leave within you one stone upon another; because you did not recognize the time of your *visitation* from God" (Luke 19:41–44).

Verse 2: 72–75
The second verse of this early Christian hymn about Jesus recalls the gracious actions of God in Israel and the promises the believers now considered fulfilled in Jesus. In this way, Luke emphasises that God is faithful. God has kept faith with Israel, "our ancestors", and now will keep faith with "us" and rescue us from "the hands of our enemies".

Verse 3: 76–77
While the previous verses have had their focus on Jesus, the Davidic messiah, the next verse turns to the child in the hands of Zechariah. For this reason, scholars consider that these verses have been added by Luke in order to make use of this early Christian hymn in its current context. The neighbours had asked, "What then will this child become?", and now Zechariah looks toward the future ministry of John as one who prepares the way for Jesus and one whose ministry will be the forgiveness of sin through ritual immersion (baptism).

Conclusion: 78–79
These verses return to the theme of God's visitation: a visitation of tender compassion, bringing light to those sitting in darkness awaiting death.

The early Christians knew this darkness when faced by opposition from Roman local authorities and then the persecutions of Nero (64–68 CE).

Zechariah's Canticle of Praise (Author's Translation)

⁶⁷ Then his father Zechariah was filled with the Holy Spirit and spoke this prophecy:
⁶⁸ "Blessed be the Lord God of Israel,

Verse 1:
for he has visited his people and redeemed them. ⁶⁹ God has raised up a mighty saviour for us in the house of his servant David, ⁷⁰ as spoken through the mouth of holy prophets from of old, ⁷¹ that we would be saved from our enemies and from the hand of all who hate us.

Verse 2
⁷² Thus God has shown the mercy promised to our ancestors, and has remembered the holy covenant, ⁷³ the oath that was sworn to our ancestor Abraham, to grant us ⁷⁴ that we, being rescued from the hands of our enemies, might serve God without fear, ⁷⁵ in holiness and righteousness before him all our days.

Verse 3 (an addition by Luke)
⁷⁶ And you, child, will be called the prophet of the Most High; for you will go before the Lord to prepare his ways, ⁷⁷ to give knowledge of salvation to his people by the forgiveness of their sins.

Conclusion
⁷⁸ By the tender mercy of our God, the dawn from on high will visit us, ⁷⁹ to give light to those who sit in darkness and in the shadow of death, to guide our feet into the way of peace." ⁸⁰ The child grew and became strong in spirit, and he was in the wilderness until the day he appeared publicly to Israel.

THE BIRTH OF JESUS – MOVING BEYOND THE CHRISTMAS PAGEANTS

Before examining Luke's narrative of Jesus' birth, it would be helpful to clear up some misunderstandings that we have unconsciously inherited from Christmas pageants, carols and celebrations as a child.

Top: Nativity scene in St Peter's church, Ghent, Belgium.

Opposite page (top): Augustus, Victorian engraving.

Opposite page (bottom): Icon of Jesus, Hagia Sophia, Istanbul, Turkey.

DECEMBER 25 (FIRST CELEBRATED IN 336 CE)

Luke does not record the date of Jesus' birth, although he does give some clues. The date December 25 was established during the time of the Emperor Constantine when he accepted Christianity for his empire. In pagan Rome, this date, at the time of the winter solstice in the northern hemisphere, was considered to be the birth of the sun following the darkness of winter. From this time the daylight gradually increases. The festival was called "*Sol Invictus*" – the invincible sun. After Constantine's rule, the festival seems to have changed its focus from the rebirth of the sun to the birth of the Son of God, and so Christmas day was established.

BORN IN A STABLE

The idea of a stable outside a house is a very European idea. Poorer houses in ancient Israel usually kept their small flock inside their house during the winter nights to protect the sheep from bitter frosts. The warmth of the animals would also provide extra warmth for the families.

NO ROOM IN THE "INN"

The word used by Luke and translated "inn" actually means a place where one's sleeping blanket would be rolled out on the floor of the house. Houses were very simple, with just one room, and sleeping mats would be rolled out on the floor at night. This is where the family would all sleep.

LAID IN A MANGER

Luke has Jesus born in a part of the house where animals were usually kept and then describes Jesus sleeping in a "manger", which is a feeding trough for animals.

Luke tells us that there was no room in the usual sleeping place for the family, which is why Mary has her child in a smaller area inside and towards the rear of the house kept for a few sheep or goats.

When we read the biblical episodes, we need to be alert to the fact that we are reading about a very different time and culture, and we can make mistakes if we imagine that the biblical world is like our world today.

THE BIRTH OF A SAVIOUR – JESUS OR AUGUSTUS

Augustus

The narrative returns to the power of Rome, the emperor and governor. From the previous chapter we also know that Jesus was born during the reign of Herod. These three facts need to be carefully examined when considering the time of Jesus birth.

> Augustus was Emperor from 27 BCE to 14 CE. Quirinius was governor of Syria from 6 –7 CE when he conducted a census of Judea (not Galilee).
>
> But Herod died in 4 BCE.

It seems that Luke, writing seventy to eighty years later, has confused the time of Quirinius as governor, back-dating his rule to a time when Herod lived.

It is more likely that Jesus was born at the end of the reign of Herod i.e. 6–4 BCE.

By naming a census, even if Luke has incorrect timing, he provides a reason for Mary and Joseph to travel down from Nazareth to Bethlehem. Here, Luke assumes that Joseph and Mary lived in Nazareth but Jesus was born in Bethlehem.

The birthday of Augustus

Considering Luke's announcement of the birth of Jesus, it is also worth noting an inscription found in Prieme (Turkey) establishing the date for celebrating the Emperor's birthday.

> It seemed good to the Greeks of Asia … "Since Providence … has set in most perfect order by giving us Augustus, … sending him as a **saviour**, both for us and for our descendants, that he might end war and arrange all things, and since he, Caesar, by his appearance (*epiphany*) … and since the **birthday of**

THE BIRTH OF JESUS

In those days a decree went out from Emperor Augustus that all the world should be registered. ²This was the first registration and was taken while Quirinius was governor of Syria. ³All went to their own towns to be registered. ⁴Joseph also went from the town of Nazareth in Galilee to Judea, to the city of David called Bethlehem, because he was descended from the house and family of David. ⁵He went to be registered with Mary, to whom he was engaged and who was expecting a child. ⁶While they were there, the time came for her to deliver her child. ⁷And she gave birth to her firstborn son and wrapped him in bands of cloth, and laid him in a manger, because there was no place for them in the sleeping area.⁸ In that region there were shepherds living in the fields, keeping watch over their flock by night. ⁹Then an angel of the Lord stood before them, and the glory of the Lord shone around them, and they were terrified. ¹⁰But the angel said to them, "Do not be afraid; for see—I am bringing you **good tidings** of great joy for **all the people**: ¹¹to you is born this day in the city of David a **Saviour,** who is the Messiah, the Lord. ¹²This will be a sign for you: you will find a child wrapped in bands of cloth and lying in a manger." ¹³And suddenly there was with the angel a multitude of the heavenly host, praising God, and saying,
¹⁴ "Glory to God in the highest heaven, and on earth **peace** among those whom he favors!"
(Luke 2:1–14)

Below: Snow in Jerusalem in December.

Opposite page (left): When the crops had been harvested, the sheep were then permitted in the fields, where they ate the stubble and, most importantly, their droppings provided fertiliser for the next harvest. That sheep are in the fields at night suggests that Luke situates these scenes following the grain harvest, perhaps in May.

Opposite page (right): Sheep would usually graze on the side of rugged hills and certainly not in carefully tended *fields* where farmers guarded their crops, often behind stone fences.

the god Augustus was the beginning of the good tidings for the world that came by reason of him" which Asia resolved in Smyrna (Excerpt from the Priene Inscription).

The Prieme inscription (9 BCE) announces Augustus as a worldwide saviour who ended all war and established peace after years of civil war. This is the *Pax Augustae*, considered to be good tidings for the whole world. For this, Augustus is hailed as a god. Luke contradicts this by proclaiming a *Pax Christi* and good news (*evangelia*) in the form of a Saviour ushering in peace on earth. This Saviour is announced to the little ones, the shepherds, and can be found in an animal's feeding trough, a manger. This is a sign that Jesus' mission is to be for the poor and oppressed.

LUKE'S CLUES TO THE TIME OF JESUS' BIRTH

It has been explained why December 25 was established during the time of Emperor Constantine as the date for Christmas: to replace the pagan festival of *Sol Invictus*. Luke does provide other clues.

Luke writes, "In that region there were shepherds living in the fields, keeping watch over their flock by night" (2:8). Some important terms to notice: the shepherds are in the fields at night.

For this to have any accuracy, the climate in the hills around Bethlehem had to be temperate, not the frosty nights found in December, when it occasionally snows.

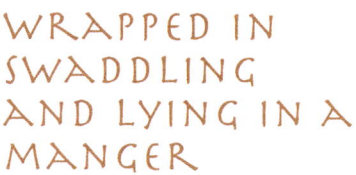

WRAPPED IN SWADDLING AND LYING IN A MANGER

Following the angelic message, the shepherds respond by going to Bethlehem to see the sign that had been spoken of: "a child wrapped in bands of cloth and lying in a manger".

This is the third time that Luke has written of a "manger". While it suggests the poverty of a family needing to lay their newborn in a feeding trough, Luke more likely has a verse from the Old Testament in mind.

Centuries earlier, the prophet Isaiah had written,

> Hear, O heavens, and listen, O earth; for the LORD has spoken: I reared children and brought them up, but they have rebelled against me. The ox knows its owner, and the donkey its master's manger; but Israel does not know, my people do not understand (Isa 1:2–3).

Here God is charging the people of Israel with rebellion. They are like children who have been fed and raised by a parent but then turn against their parent. Even animals know who feeds them and can recognise the manger from where they receive food. By using the term "manger" three times, Luke alludes to these verses. Not only does this allusion support Luke's theology that Jesus fulfils the Old Testament prophecies, but it also offers some explanation as to why many within Israel did not acknowledge Jesus when they should have recognised their Lord. This too, for some mysterious reason, was part of God's plan and foretold by Isaiah.

In Luke's birth narrative there is probably also an allusion to David's son Solomon, who says in the book of Wisdom:

> And when I was born,
> I began to breathe the common air, and fell upon the kindred earth;
> my first sound was a cry, as is true of all. I was nursed with care in swaddling cloths.
> For no king has had a different beginning of existence (Wis 7:3–5).

Jesus is born into the House of David, and, although born in poverty, in his adult ministry he will be hailed as King when he enters Jerusalem:

> Blessed is the king who comes in the name of the Lord! Peace in heaven, and glory in the highest heaven! (Luke 19:38)

THE SIGN FOR THE SHEPHERDS

¹⁵ When the angels had left them and gone into heaven, the shepherds said to one another, "Let us go now to Bethlehem and see this thing that has taken place, which the Lord has made known to us." ¹⁶ So they went with haste and found Mary and Joseph, and the child lying in the manger. ¹⁷ When they saw this, they made known what had been told them about this child; ¹⁸ and all who heard it were amazed at what the shepherds told them. ¹⁹ But Mary treasured all these words and pondered them in her heart. ²⁰ The shepherds returned, glorifying and praising God for all they had heard and seen, as it had been told them (Luke 2:15–21).

THE CIRCUMCISION AND PRESENTATION IN THE TEMPLE

The circumcision on the eighth day is mentioned briefly, but the presentation of Jesus, the first-born male child, in the Temple is given greater significance.

According to Jewish Law, a mother was considered ritually unclean for seven days after the birth of a child and so not permitted/expected to join in community worship. At the circumcision on the eighth day, it is the father's right to name the child, just as Zechariah named his son John. But Luke does not name Joseph in this scene; there is no father-figure at this circumcision. Instead, Luke reminds the reader that Jesus had been named by God's messenger even prior to his conception: "he was called Jesus, the name given by the angel before he was conceived in the womb." The only one Jesus calls "father" is God.

Following the circumcision, this time of purification is extended a further 33 days to give a total of 40 days, and then mother and child present themselves to the priest.

> If a woman conceives and bears a male child, she shall be ceremonially unclean seven days ...[3] On the eighth day the flesh of his foreskin shall be circumcised. [4] Her time of blood purification shall be thirty-three days; she shall not touch any holy thing, or come into the sanctuary, until the days of her purification are completed...[6] When the days of her purification are completed, she shall bring to the priest at the entrance of

Below: *Presentation of Jesus in the Temple*, by Giovanni Bellini.

the Tent of Meeting a lamb in its first year for a burnt offering …⁸ If she cannot afford a sheep, she shall take two turtledoves or two pigeons (Lev 12:1–8).

When Mary and Joseph take the child to the Temple in Jerusalem, they make the offering of a poor family of two turtledoves.

NUMBERS AND THEOLOGY

In the story of John's birth, no mention is made of his presentation after circumcision, but it is named now. In introducing the passage of the presentation of Jesus, Luke is returning to his apocalyptic theme and reliance on the book of Daniel.

> ²⁴ Seventy weeks are decreed for your people and your holy city: to finish the transgression, to put an end to sin, and to atone for iniquity, to bring in everlasting righteousness, to seal both vision and prophet, and to anoint a most holy place.²⁵ Know therefore and understand: from the time that the word went out to restore and rebuild Jerusalem until the time of an anointed prince [in Greek a *Christos*], there shall be seven weeks; and for sixty-two weeks it shall be built again with streets and moat, but in a troubled time. ²⁶ After the sixty-two weeks, an anointed one [*christos*] shall be cut off and shall have nothing, and the troops of the prince who is to come shall destroy the city and the sanctuary. Its end shall come with a flood, and to the end there shall be war. Desolations are decreed. ²⁷ He shall make a strong covenant with many for one week, and for half of the week he shall make sacrifice and offering cease; and in their place shall be an abomination that desolates, until the decreed end is poured out upon the desolator (Daniel 9:24–27).

Look at the significant time indicators in this passage:

> A total of 70 weeks of years = 70 x 7 = 490 years before the end-time.

In the infancy narrative, Luke has very carefully named certain lengths of time.

> The annunciation happens in the sixth month of Elizabeth's pregnancy, i.e.
> 6 x 30 days = 180 days.
>
> Mary has nine months pregnancy until the birth of Jesus
> 9 x 30 days = 270 days
>
> Following the birth there are 40 days until the presentation of Jesus in the Temple.
> 40 days
>
> The total number of days from the time of the annunciation of Jesus until his presentation
> = 490 days.

In the scene of his presentation, Jesus is named as the Lord's anointed one: in Hebrew, the *Messiah*, and in Greek, the *Christos*.

These aspects of Luke's narrative provide clues about his theology and interpretation of the adult Jesus. Jesus is the *Christos*/anointed one ushering the end days and the reign of God as prophesied by Daniel.

> ## PRESENTATION OF JESUS IN THE TEMPLE
>
> ²¹ After eight days had passed, it was time to circumcise the child; and he was called Jesus, the name given by the angel before he was conceived in the womb. ²² When the time came for their purification according to the law of Moses, they brought him up to Jerusalem to present him to the Lord ²³ (as it is written in the law of the Lord, "Every firstborn male shall be designated as holy to the Lord"), ²⁴ and they offered a sacrifice according to what is stated in the law of the Lord, "a pair of turtledoves or two young pigeons." ²⁵ Now there was a man in Jerusalem whose name was Simeon; this man was righteous and devout, looking forward to the consolation of Israel, and the Holy Spirit rested on him. ²⁶ It had been revealed to him by the Holy Spirit that he would not see death before he had seen the Lord's Messiah. ²⁷ Guided by the Spirit, Simeon came into the temple; and when the parents brought in the child Jesus, to do for him what was customary under the law, Simeon took him in his arms and praised God, saying, ²⁹ "Master, now you are dismissing your servant in peace, according to your word; ³⁰ for my eyes have seen your salvation, ³¹ which you have prepared in the presence of all peoples, ³² a light for revelation to the Gentiles and for glory to your people Israel" (Luke 2:21–32).

Above: *Simeon's Song of Praise*, by Rembrandt van Rijn.

THE CANTICLE OF SIMEON: THE TEMPLE OF GOD'S GLORY REVEALED

Simeon and Anna have their background in the Old Testament story of Eli and Hannah (Anna), who were the parents of the prophet Samuel. The two prophets, a man and a woman, neatly balance the opening scene with Zechariah and Elizabeth (1:1–25).

Jesus' parents fulfilled the Jewish Law, mentioned three times in the purification scene. When Simeon is introduced, the Holy Spirit is mentioned three times, establishing him as a prophet, and Anna is also called a "prophet" (v. 36). The Law and the Prophets is a way of referring to the whole scriptural heritage of Israel, and this heritage has now come together and focused on Jesus. In this way, Luke reassures his community about God's fidelity and that the Jesus story is in continuity with the great story of Israel.

In a sense, Simeon stands for Israel – described as righteous and devout and even in his old age awaiting the Messiah. Now he sees and recognises in Jesus that the promise has been fulfilled. Now he can go in peace.

During the time of Israel's exile in Babylon (587–537 BCE), the prophet Isaiah had assured Israel that God had not deserted them and would come to save them. His oracles begin with the words,

"Comfort, O comfort my people" (Isa 40:1). This Isaiah theme of consolation is accompanied by the promise that the Gentiles will stream to Jerusalem and the glory of God that once filled the Temple will be restored. Simeon, representing Israel, now sees this promise of consolation fulfilled. His Canticle echoes many of the verses from Isaiah.

> The LORD has bared his holy arm before the eyes of all the Gentiles; and all the ends of the earth shall see the salvation of our God (Isa 52:10). "I will give you as a light to the nations, that my salvation may reach to the end of the earth" (Isa 49:6). "Then the glory of the LORD shall be revealed, and all people shall see it together…" (Isa 40:5).

PROPHETS IN THE TEMPLE

³³And the child's father and mother were amazed at what was being said about him. ³⁴ Then Simeon blessed them and said to his mother Mary, "This child is destined for the falling and the rising of many in Israel, and to be a sign that will be opposed ³⁵ so that the inner thoughts of many will be revealed—and a sword will pierce your own soul too." ³⁶ There was also a prophet, Anna the daughter of Phanuel, of the tribe of Asher. She was of a great age, having lived with her husband seven years after her marriage, ³⁷ then as a widow to the age of eighty-four. She never left the temple but worshiped there with fasting and prayer night and day. ³⁸ At that moment she came, and began to praise God and to speak about the child to all who were looking for the redemption of Jerusalem. ³⁹ When they had finished everything required by the law of the Lord, they returned to Galilee, to their own town of Nazareth. ⁴⁰ The child grew and became strong, filled with wisdom; and the favor of God was upon him (Luke 2:33–40).

PROPHETS IN THE TEMPLE: GOD IS FAITHFUL

Notice how important the Temple is within Luke's infancy narrative; later this importance will continue in the Gospel narrative. The Gospel opens in the Temple, and at the end of the Gospel, Jesus asks his disciples to stay in Jerusalem. Luke tells us, "The disciples worshiped him, and returned to Jerusalem with great joy; and they were continually in the temple blessing God" (Luke 24:52–53).

By the time of Luke's writing, the Temple had been destroyed and the earlier Gospels offered an interpretation of this event, so tragic for Judaism. The Temple was either to be replaced by the community of disciples, making a new "house of prayer for all people" (Mark 11:17), or rebuilt in the person of Jesus (Emmanuel) present "until the end of the age" (Matt 28:28). In Luke, the Temple is presented positively, both within the infancy narratives and then within the Gospel. But in the Acts of the Apostles, Paul travels to Jerusalem and the Temple closes its doors on him (Acts 21:30). Luke offers his community an interpretation of the destruction of Jerusalem: that God has kept faith with Israel, offering first Jesus, who was rejected, and then a second chance through the preaching of the disciples, but this was also rejected.

Simeon's final words speak of the future "falling and rising" of Israel as people respond to Jesus' ministry. Some will accept his "good news", but some will oppose him. Even before the adult ministry begins, Luke has introduced the theme of acceptance and conflict that Jesus will experience, thus preparing the reader for the following narrative.

ARCHAEOLOGY AT NAZARETH

In 1884, a workman accidentally broke through into a large cavern underneath a convent in Nazareth. This opened up for the first time the remains of a series of buildings that had lain buried since crusader times. The only hint of something beneath was the oral memory of the people. A neighbour told the sisters, when they were buying the property in 1855, "Be careful, my land is holy ground. This is where the saint is buried." The woman then bent, touched the ground with her fingers, and then kissed them. The oral memory kept alive what had been lost and buried.

Archaeologists have now unearthed a first-century house and, right next to it, a very early Jewish Christian church, known by pilgrims as "the Church of the Nutrition". This was the main church in Nazareth, as described by a Bishop Arculf (670). The archaeologists also found a male skeleton, buried beneath this church in a sitting position with a ring on his finger. This finding suggests that this was the bishop of Nazareth upon his chair (*kathedra*).

The placing of this church next to this house, the importance of the "cathedral" church of a bishop, and its name, "Church of the Nutrition", have led to the belief that this house was once the home in Nazareth of Jesus, Mary and Joseph.

JESUS IN THE TEMPLE

Luke adds a story about Jesus' childhood, recounting the time when Jesus goes with his parents to Jerusalem to celebrate the Jewish feast of Passover. The small detail that Jesus was about twelve years old suggests that this was the age when a young boy was recognised as an adult in the Jewish community.

Top: This stone from Abu Gosh commemorates a detachment (*vexillatio*) of the Roman Tenth Legion, which took part in the Jewish war resulting in the destruction of Jerusalem. It was known as the Tenth Fretensi and this stone reads VEXILLATIO LEG X FRE.

Bottom: Deep under the house in Nazareth is a first-century rolling stone tomb – could this be the tomb of the "saint", the tomb of Joseph? The people kept the memory of this site for centuries, revering its holiness above any other place in Nazareth.

DID YOU KNOW?

✦ Today a Jewish boy participates in a ceremony called a Bar Mitzvah (Son of the Covenant) when he is around twelve. During this ceremony, he reads the scriptures for the first time and from then on he is considered an adult and able to fully participate in Jewish worship.

✦ Before he can take part in this ceremony, a young boy has to study the scripture passages and learn about his responsibilities.

✦ In some communities a similar ceremony happens for a young girl; this is called a Bat Mitzvah (Daughter of the Covenant).

In Luke's story, Jesus stays behind in Jerusalem for some days. When Mary and Joseph find him, he is in the Temple sitting among the teachers, listening to them as a student and asking them questions. In this story we catch a glimpse of Jesus learning the traditions of his people from the Jewish rabbis, just as any young person has to learn from teachers.

Jesus' mother says to him, "Son, why have you treated us so? Behold, your father and I have been looking for you anxiously." Jesus replies, "Did you not know that I must be about my Father's business?"

Here, Luke gives us a clue to Jesus' real identity – although he is thought to be the son of Joseph and Mary, Jesus' true Father is God. The infancy narrative concludes, very clearly indicating Jesus' vocation: to be about his Father's business.

Top: The star marks the place of Jesus' birth in the Church of the Nativity, Bethlehem.

Bottom: *Christ in the Temple*, by Heinrich Hofman.

Opposite page: A model of the temple built by Herod over many years. The entry would be from the gates on the left-hand side. The gate in the foreground leads out to Mount of Olives. On the right, with the four towers, is the Roman Antonia fortress. The Temple towered over the rest of Jerusalem. Gentiles were permitted in the outer courts up to a barrier to the left and right of the central building.

BOY JESUS IN THE TEMPLE AT PASSOVER

[41] Now every year his parents went to Jerusalem for the festival of the Passover. [42] And when he was twelve years old, they went up as usual for the festival. [43] When the festival was ended and they started to return, the boy Jesus stayed behind in Jerusalem, but his parents did not know it. [44] Assuming that he was in the group of travellers, they went a day's journey. Then they started to look for him among their relatives and friends. [45] When they did not find him, they returned to Jerusalem to search for him. [46] After three days they found him in the temple, sitting among the teachers, listening to them and asking them questions. [47] And all who heard him were amazed at his understanding and his answers. [48] When his parents saw him they were astonished; and his mother said to him, "Child, why have you treated us like this? Look, your father and I have been searching for you in great anxiety." [49] He said to them, "Why were you searching for me? Did you not know that I must be about my Father's business?" [50] But they did not understand what he said to them. [51] Then he went down with them and came to Nazareth, and was obedient to them. His mother treasured all these things in her heart. [52] And Jesus increased in wisdom and in years, and in divine and human favor (Luke 2:41–52).

CONCLUSION: SEEKING A DEEPER MEANING

In these pages you have come to know some of the deeper meaning of the birth stories of Jesus. Where Mark began his Gospel with the adult Jesus, both Matthew and Luke introduced the adult Jesus by means of these two different infancy narratives. For both evangelists we can detect the basic oral memory: Jesus was born in Bethlehem during the time of Herod the Great, but then grew up in Nazareth; his parents were known as Joseph and Mary. Both evangelists then draw upon the literary styles of the first century and the scriptures of Israel to bring out the deeper meaning of this birth. Because these evangelists now live in the time of the Risen Christ, for them, the adult life of Jesus is over. His death is in the past, but his glorious resurrection and power of the Holy Spirit is their present experience of God. In the light of this present experience of the power of God, they tell the birth of Jesus to teach their readers that God had always been present and working in the life of this child, from the moment of his conception. Using genealogy, midrash, the form of an announcement story and symbols, the evangelists created these narratives that would have spoken to their audiences with joy and hope. They were not living in a scientific age looking for facts, but a religious age looking for meaning.

Matthew, writing for a community that had their origins in Judaism, looks back to the story of Moses to shape his story of Jesus. Then, through the Scripture citations, Matthew shows that Israel's history and the ancient prophecies have now been fulfilled. Jesus is a new Moses, with new teaching and a new covenant, forming a new people of God.

Luke, writing for a community of Gentiles – some of whom may have known and been attracted to Judaism – shows that God's Spirit has been at work from the dawn of creation, through the people of Israel and now through Jesus. This good news of salvation is for all people, especially for the "little ones" who know poverty or failure.

To appreciate these narratives as adults today, we need to enter into the religious wonder of the original readers and suspend our scientific, historical desires to know – exactly what happened, when and where. There is mystery in the birth of any child – and especially one known as the child of God.

In summary, the birth stories were told to introduce the adult Jesus and to reveal who Jesus was and what his mission would be.

✦ These two different stories were written for two different communities – one Jewish-Christian (Matthew) and one Gentile-Christian (Luke). This has an effect on the symbols used and the different approaches taken.

✦ The birth stories connect Jesus with his Jewish ancestors and their history.

✦ In order to understand Jesus, we need to know some information about the Old Testament and the traditions of Israel.

✦ These birth stories were written in the way that fitted the pattern of birth stories two thousand years ago, not the way that we are used to in current times.

✦ The historical details such as Mary, Joseph, Caesar Augustus, Herod and Quirinius match what is known from Roman and Jewish sources.

✦ Other symbolic details describe truthful aspects of the adult Jesus' life – e.g. his care for the poor and outcasts and his announcing that the reign of God has begun.

✦ Some details remain shrouded in mystery.

FURTHER READING

Brown, Raymond E. *An Adult Christ at Christmas*. Collegeville: Liturgical Press, 1975.

Brown, Raymond E. *The Birth of the Messiah*. Garden City: Doubleday, 1979.

Hendrickx, Herman. *The Infancy Narratives*. Manila: East Asian Pastoral Institute, 1975.

YouTube video on the infancy narratives:

https:www.youtube.com/watch?v=KIdm9u42ES4&list=PLEsiOGKIC3U6MDq59zEIniHU-F2E8ame0h&index=4

A YouTube video about the discovery of Herod's tomb can be viewed at: https://www.youtube.com/watch?v=IrjAXnCW4FQ

www.ingramcontent.com/pod-product-compliance
Lightning Source LLC
Chambersburg PA
CBHW061059170426
43199CB00025B/2936